DESSERTS

DESSERTS

Classic step-by-step Cookery Collection

GINA STEER
COOKERY EDITOR OF WOMAN'S OWN

HAMLYN

First published 1992
Hamlyn is an imprint of
Octopus Illustrated Publishing,
part of Reed International Books Limited,
Michelin House, 81 Fulham Road,
London, SW3 6RB

Text and illustrations © 1992 IPC
Magazines Limited
Design © 1992 Reed International
Books Limited

A catalogue record for this book is
available from the British Library

ISBN 0 600 57566 7

Produced by Mandarin Offset
Printed and Bound in Hong Kong

NOTES

Both metric and imperial measurements have been used in all recipes.
Use one set of measurements only and not a mixture of both.

Standard level spoon measurements are used in all recipes
1 tablespoon = one 15 ml spoon
1 teaspoon = one 5 ml spoon

Ovens should be preheated to the specific temperature.
If using a fan assisted oven, follow manufacturer's instructions
for adjusting the temperature.

This book is a must for all those, who like me, have a sweet tooth and like to indulge every once in a while. Whereas the recipes are not all 'naughty' some are just plain 'wicked', but why not? We all deserve a treat every once in a while.

There's a dessert to suit everyone in this collection of delicious recipes. You can choose from Profiteroles with a velvety thick chocolate sauce, or a luscious Chocolate Roulade, that's really wicked but quite irresistible for all those avid chocoholics. For those who have an exceptionally sweet tooth, try a couple of slices of Hazelnut Vacherin or a pot or two of Crème Brûlée. Plus there are the desserts for the slightly more adventurous: Croquembouche, the classic French Wedding Cake – a stunning centrepiece for any occasion, or a spectacular Mount Vesuvius dessert or even an Iced Orange Bowl which is guaranteed to give you a standing ovation.

As well as all the more exotic desserts, no book would be complete without some everyday puds which are real family favourites and just right for those winter days when you need some comfort food. Try a slice of Jam Roly Poly that's oozing with jam or good old-fashioned Spotted Dick that's laden with currants and a subtle hint of lemon. Apple Dumplings or an Apple Pie will get the whole family just asking for more and an absolute must that's a rib sticking treat, Bread Pudding, served hot or cold, mmmmm... superb!

As with the other books in this series, all the recipes have been thoroughly tested in the Woman's Own test kitchen so you can cook them with absolute confidence, knowing that they will work every time. As an added bonus we've also included a handy tip on each and every recipe just to give you all a little more information or help. I am sure you will get as much pleasure from this book as as I did from writing it.

I hope you enjoy the book.

Happy cooking

Gina Steer

Gina Steer

CREME CARAMEL

This delicious dessert is a combination of smooth, creamy egg custard, coated in a delicious golden caramel sauce, and is really simple to make when you follow this easy, step-by-step guide. Serve it chilled with fresh fruit, biscuits and cream.

Calories per portion: 257   **SERVES 4**

4½ oz/120 g caster sugar
3 eggs, size 3
¾ pint/450 ml milk
½ tsp vanilla essence
whitecurrants to decorate

Preheat the oven to Gas 3, 325°F, 160°C. Place 4 oz/100 g caster sugar and ¼ pint/150 ml water in a heavy-based pan. Place pan over a gentle heat, and stir until the sugar has dissolved. Bring to the boil and boil vigorously for about 8-10 mins until a golden caramel has been formed.

While boiling the caramel, you should have ready a pastry brush and a measuring jug filled with cold water. As a sugar crust begins to form around the pan, just above the level of the syrup, dip the pastry brush into the cold water and use to push the crust from the sides of the pan down into the boiling liquid caramel.

Having made the caramel, pour it into a 6 in/15 cm soufflé or ovenproof dish. Using oven gloves or a cloth, rotate the dish carefully, so that the caramel coats the base and sides of the dish. Take care not to burn yourself with the hot caramel. Put the dish to one side while preparing the custard.

Whisk the eggs and remaining sugar together. Warm the milk to blood heat (this is when a clean finger dipped into the milk feels just warm), then gradually whisk into the egg and sugar mixture. Stir in the vanilla essence then, using a sieve, carefully strain the custard mixture into the caramel-lined soufflé dish. Place dish in a roasting tin, filled with sufficient hot water to come halfway up the sides of the dish.

Place in the centre of the oven and cook for approx 1 hr or until set and firm to the touch. (To check if the custard is set, carefully insert a round-bladed knife into the centre – if the knife is completely dry when you remove it and no liquid seeps out, the custard is ready. Remove from the oven, cool, then chill overnight in the fridge.

Remove from fridge 30 mins before serving. To turn out, using your fingertip, loosen the outside edge of the custard carefully. Place a serving dish over the top, then invert the dish, shaking slightly if necessary. Leave the soufflé dish on inverted top until all the caramel has drained out. Decorate and serve with fresh fruit, cream and home-made biscuits.

HANDY TIP

Make individual puddings using four ¼ pint/150 ml ramekin dishes. Proceed as above then cook for 25-35 mins or until set.

1. Stir caster sugar and water over a gentle heat until the sugar has dissolved

2. Brush sugar crust from the sides of the pan down into the boiling caramel

3. Swirl the caramel round a 6 in/15 cm soufflé dish, to coat the base and sides

4. Beat the eggs and remaining sugar, then gradually whisk in the warmed milk

5. Using a sieve, strain custard mixture into the caramel-lined soufflé dish

6. Place dish in a tin filled with hot water to come halfway up sides, then cook

SULTANA CHEESECAKE

This tempting cheesecake is crammed full of sun-ripened sultanas, with creamy ricotta cheese that's been flavoured with orange and encased in an orangey pastry then topped with tangy sweet currants.

Calories per portion: 502   **SERVES 12**

FOR THE PASTRY:
10 oz/300 g plain flour
5 oz/150 g butter or margarine
1 oz/25 g sugar
grated rind 1 orange
1 egg yolk, size 3
2-3 tbsp orange juice
FOR THE FILLING:
1½ lb/675 g ricotta cheese
4 oz/100 g caster sugar
1 orange
3 eggs, size 3
8 fl oz/250 ml double cream
4 oz/100 g sultanas
FOR THE TOPPING:
10 oz/300 g red and
   blackcurrants, thawed if
   frozen, cleaned if fresh
3 oz/75 g caster sugar
2 tsp arrowroot

Preheat oven to Gas 4, 350°F, 180°C, 10 mins before baking the cheesecake. To prepare the pastry, sieve the flour into a mixing bowl, then add the fat. Mix in the sugar and orange rind then rub the fat in until the mixture resembles fine breadcrumbs. Add the egg yolk and orange juice and mix to form a smooth and pliable dough. Knead lightly on a floured surface then wrap and chill leave to relax for 30 mins. Roll out and use to completely line an 8½ in/21.5 cm spring form tin. Leave in the fridge while preparing the filling.

To prepare filling, push the ricotta cheese through a fine sieve into a bowl and add the sugar. Finely grate the rind

from the orange and squeeze out the juice. Add the orange rind to the bowl and beat well until the mixture is smooth. Gradually add the eggs, beating well between each addition to ensure the mixture remains smooth, then stir in the orange juice and lastly the double cream. Fold in the sultanas. Pour the mixture into the pastry-lined tin then bake in the oven for 1½ hrs or until the cheesecake is firm to the touch. Turn the oven off and leave the cheesecake in for ½ hr. Remove from the oven, allow to cool then chill for at least 4 hrs, preferably overnight.

To make the topping, lightly wash the currants if using fresh. Drain well. Dissolve the sugar in 4 tbsp of water then boil for 5 mins. Remove from the heat and add the currants. Return to the heat. Blend the arrowroot with 2 tsp of cold water then stir into the fruit. Cook stirring until the mixture clears and thickens. Remove from heat and allow to cool. Remove the cheesecake from the tin and if necessary trim the top of the pastry to form a neat edge. Spoon the prepared topping over then leave for 2 hrs to set. Serve if liked with cream.

HANDY TIP

Vary the topping according to taste and availability of the fruit – why not try coarsely grated chocolate or chocolate curls for a real treat, then dust top lightly with sieved icing sugar.

1. Place flour in bowl with the sugar and fat, add grated orange rind. Rub in until mixture resembles breadcrumbs

2. Roll the pastry out on a lightly floured surface then use to line an 8½ in/21.5 cm spring form tin

3. Push the ricotta cheese through a fine sieve into a bowl, add the sugar and finely grated orange rind. Beat well

4. Beat the mixture together until smooth then gradually add the eggs, beating well after each addition

5. Stir in the orange juice, the double cream and lastly fold in the sultanas. Mix lightly together

6. Pour the mixture into the pastry-lined case then bake in the oven for 1½ hrs, or until firm to the touch

MARBLED PUDDING

For an old-fashioned family treat, get steaming this wonderfully scrumptious chocolate and vanilla pud! It is best served with lashings of home-made, creamy custard sauce.

Calories per portion: 633   SERVES 6

6 oz/175 g softened butter or margarine

6 oz/175 g caster sugar

3 eggs, size 3

6 oz/175 g self-raising flour

¼ tsp vanilla essence

1½ oz/40 g plain chocolate, melted

1½ oz/40 g chocolate chips

FOR THE CUSTARD SAUCE:

1 oz/25 g caster sugar or to taste

2 tbsp cornflour

3 egg yolks, size 3

¾ pint/450 ml milk

2 tsp vanilla essence

2 tbsp extra thick double cream, optional

Lightly grease and line a 2 pint/1.2 litre pudding basin. Place softened butter or margarine and sugar in a mixing bowl and beat until pale and fluffy.

Beat the eggs together and add gradually to the mixture, beating well after each addition. If the mixture begins to separate out add a little of the flour. Sieve the flour into the bowl and, using a metal spoon, gently fold the flour into the mixture in a figure of eight movement.

Divide the mixture in two and place

HANDY TIP

Try serving the pudding with a toffee sauce: melt 8 oz/225 g vanilla toffees with 7 fl oz/200 ml milk and 1 oz/25 g butter, stir well and use immediately.

---

in two separate bowls. Flavour one with vanilla essence and add 1 tbsp tepid boiled water; flavour the other with the melted chocolate and chocolate chips and add 1 tbsp tepid boiled water. Gently mix to form a soft dropping consistency.

Spoon the mixture alternately into the prepared basin and, using a fork, gently blend some of the mixture together forming a marbled effect.

Cover the surface of the mixture with a disc of greaseproof paper. Pleat a sheet of greaseproof paper and place over the basin, securing with string. Cover this with foil.

Stand the basin in a large saucepan, pour in enough water to come 3 in/7.5 cm up the side of the basin and bring to the boil. Alternatively, place in the top of a steamer over a pan of gently simmering water. Cover and steam for 1½ -2 hrs, topping up water as necessary. To check the pudding is cooked: it will have risen and a skewer inserted into the middle of the pudding will come out clean.

Meanwhile make the custard, beat together the sugar, cornflour and egg yolks. Gradually blend in the milk and pour into a heatproof bowl. Stand over a pan of simmering water and stir until thickened. Cool slightly, then stir in the vanilla and cream, if using.

To serve, remove and discard all foil and paper layers, run a palette knife around the pudding and invert on to a serving dish. Serve immediately with the custard.

1. Place softened fat and sugar in a mixing bowl and beat until pale and fluffy, then gradually beat in the eggs

2. Using a metal spoon, gently fold the flour into the mixture in a figure of eight movement

3. Flavour one with vanilla essence and the other with melted chocolate and chocolate chips

4. Spoon mixture alternately into basin. With a fork, gently blend some of mixture together forming a marbled effect

5. Pleat a sheet of greaseproof paper and place over basin, securing with string. Cover this with foil

6. Pour custard mixture into a heatproof bowl and stand over a pan of simmering water, stir until thickened.

BREAD & BUTTER PUDDING

Slices of thinly buttered bread, layered with dried fruit and almonds, with a subtle hint of orange and cooked in custard, it makes a popular family pud.

8 thin slices white bread

2 oz/50 g softened butter or low-fat spread

grated rind of 1 large orange

2 oz/50 g sultanas

2 oz/50 g seedless raisins

3 oz/75 g flaked almonds

1 oz/25 g unrefined granulated sugar

3 eggs, size 3

¾ pint/450 ml semi-skimmed milk

¼ pint/150 ml single cream

2-3 tbsp Grand Marnier, optional

2 tsp caster sugar

Preheat oven to Gas 4, 350°F, 180°C. Thinly spread the bread with the butter or low-fat spread and cut each slice diagonally into four. Use half of the bread to line the base and sides of a lightly greased 2 pint/1.2 litre oval ovenproof dish, then sprinkle with grated orange rind. Reserve the remaining bread slices.

Mix the sultanas, raisins and 2 oz/50 g of the flaked almonds together and scatter over top of bread in dish. Sprinkle with the granulated sugar. Then arrange the reserved bread across the top of the fruit.

Beat the eggs, slightly warm the milk, then beat into eggs with the cream and Grand Marnier, if using. Pour over the bread, taking care not to spill the milk over the sides of the dish. Leave to stand for at least 30 mins.

Sprinkle with remaining 1 oz/25 g flaked almonds. Place on the centre shelf of the preheated oven and bake for 45-55 mins or until the filling is lightly set and the top is golden brown and crisp. Sprinkle with caster sugar. Serve immediately with custard or cream.

For a delicious Osborne Pudding spread thin sliced brown bread with butter or low-fat spread, then with a portion of your favourite marmalade. Cut into quarters then arrange in a lightly greased ovenproof dish. Omit the fruit and nuts and use 1 oz/25 g of sugar.

Pour the beaten egg and milk over the bread and leave to stand for 30 mins before cooking as before. Sprinkle with a little demerara sugar before serving. If preferred, you can line 4-6 small ramekin dishes with the buttered bread. Proceed as above, then bake for 25-35 mins or until set.

HANDY TIPS

This pudding is ideal for using up stale bread but if the bread is really stale leave the mixture to stand a little longer before cooking.
Don't forget you can always vary the type of dried fruits or nuts according to personal taste. Try using dates, cherries, chopped no-need-to-soak apricots, mixed peel, as well as walnuts, hazelnuts, unsalted peanuts or pine kernels.
Try varying the bread as well. You can mix white and brown bread, fruit tea breads, or even malt bread or lardy cake.

1. Spread the slices of bread thinly with butter or low-fat spread

2. Cut the bread diagonally into quarters and use to line an ovenproof dish

3. With a zester remove rind from the large orange and sprinkle over the bread

4. Scatter the chopped mixed fruit, almonds and sugar over the bread

5. Warm the milk to blood heat, then whisk into the beaten eggs with liqueur

6. Pour egg mixture over pudding, leave for at least 30 mins before baking

JAM ROLY POLY

This pud must definitely be everyone's favourite!
Crisp golden suet pastry, oozing with delicious
raspberry jam. And it's not too naughty, as semi-
skimmed milk and vegetable suet have been used,
so it's a whole lot lighter on calories.

Calories per portion: 333 including custard   **SERVES 6**

6 oz/175 g self-raising flour

2 oz/50 g plain flour

a pinch of salt

1 tbsp caster sugar

3 oz/75 g vegetable suet

¼ pint/150 ml semi-skimmed
milk, plus a little extra
for brushing

2 tbsp raspberry jam, or low-
sugar raspberry conserve

1 tbsp golden caster sugar

FOR THE CUSTARD:

3 eggs, size 3

1 tbsp caster sugar

2 tsp cornflour

½ tsp vanilla essence

½ pint/300 ml semi-skimmed
milk

Preheat oven to Gas 7, 425°F, 220°C. Lightly grease a baking tray. Sift the flours, salt and caster sugar into a mixing bowl and then add the vegetable suet and mix together. Pour in the milk and mix to form a soft, but not sticky, dough. Knead lightly on a floured surface until smooth and free from cracks.

Roll the dough out to an oblong roughly 9 in x 11 in/23 cm x 28 cm. Spread the raspberry jam over the dough, leaving a 1 in/2.5 cm clear border all round. Brush the border with milk, then roll up the dough to completely enclose the jam. Pinch the ends firmly together to seal.

Place the roll, with the seam side down, on the greased baking tray. Brush with milk then sprinkle with the golden sugar.

Bake for 35-45 mins until risen and golden brown. (It is natural for a roly poly to crack along its length as it cooks.) Meanwhile, make the custard.

HANDY TIP

Try varying the flavour, by using apricot or blackcurrant jam or even marmalade.

Put the eggs, caster sugar, cornflour and vanilla essence into a bowl and mix. Heat the milk until it comes almost to the boil, then whisk it into the eggs.

Place the bowl over a saucepan of simmering water and cook, stirring continuously until the custard thickens. (Alternatively, cook the custard in a microwave oven, on High for 2½-3 mins, stirring every 30 secs with a wire whisk.) Immediately the custard thickens, pour it through a nylon sieve into a serving jug. Keep warm.

Serve the jam roly poly hot, with the custard.

1. Sift flours, salt and sugar into a mixing bowl, then add the vegetable suet

2. Add milk and mix to a soft, not sticky dough. Knead lightly until smooth

3. Roll dough on a floured surface to an oblong roughly 9 in x 11 in/23 cm x 28 cm

4. Spread jam evenly over dough with a spatula to within 1 in/2.5 cm of edge

5. Brush border with milk, then roll up from long edge. Completely tuck in ends

6. Place on baking tray, seam side down. Brush with milk, sprinkle with sugar

LEMON MERINGUE PIE

It's light and crisp with a deliciously tangy lemon filling. So it is no wonder this great melt-in-the-mouth pudding has been a favourite for years. Follow this guide, for a perfect result.

FOR THE PASTRY:
8 oz/225 g plain flour
5 oz/150 g butter or margarine
1 oz/25 g caster sugar
1 egg yolk, size 3
FOR THE FILLING:
juice and rind of 3 lemons
2 oz/50 g butter
3 oz/75 g cornflour
3 egg yolks, size 3
2-3 oz/50-75 g caster sugar
FOR THE MERINGUE:
3 egg whites, size 3
6 oz/175 g caster sugar

Preheat the oven to Gas 6, 400°F, 200°C. Place flour in a mixing bowl and rub in the butter or margarine until mixture resembles fine breadcrumbs. Stir in the sugar, beat egg yolk with 1 tbsp cold water then use to bind the pastry. Knead until smooth, wrap in greaseproof paper or clearwrap and chill for 30 mins.

Roll pastry out on a lightly floured surface and use to line a 9 in/23 cm loose-bottomed flan tin. Place a sheet of greaseproof paper in the base and cover with baking beans. Bake blind for 10-12 mins. Remove the greaseproof paper and baking beans and discard. Return the flan to the oven for a further 3-5 mins.

Make up the juice of 3 lemons to 1¼ pints/750 ml with water. Place in saucepan with the lemon rind and the butter. Bring to the boil. Blend the cornflour with 4 tbsp of water then stir into the boiling liquid. Cook over a gentle heat for 2 mins or until it is thickened.

Allow the liquid to cool then beat in the egg yolks and sugar. Pour into flan case. Return to the oven for 8-10 mins, or until the filling is set.

Whisk the egg whites until stiff and standing in peaks then add half the sugar and whisk until very stiff. Fold in the remaining sugar. Place the mixture in a piping bag fitted with a large star nozzle and pipe over the top or swirl on top of the flan with a spoon. Reduce the oven temperature to Gas 3, 325°F, 160°C, and bake the lemon meringue pie for a further 25-30 mins. Serve either hot or cold.

HANDY TIP

For an alternative filling, try chocolate. Melt 4 oz/100 g plain chocolate in a bowl over a pan of gently simmering water. Allow to cool. Leaving out the lemon juice and rind, beat the chocolate into the thickened cornflour mixture (use same quantities of water and cornflour as for lemon filling). Add the butter, cool, then beat in egg yolks and sugar. Pour into the flan case and proceed as for Lemon Meringue Pie.

1. Make pastry, chill, roll out and use to line flan tin. Bake blind

2. Assemble ingredients for the filling, make and pour into the baked flan case

3. Whisk egg whites until stiff (tip up bowl and meringue should not move)

4. Add half the sugar, whisk until very stiff, then add the remaining sugar

5. Swirl meringue topping on to flan, using back of spoon, lift upwards to form peaks

6. Lower oven temperature, return flan to the oven and bake for 25-30 mins

APPLE PIE

It's everybody's favourite – just like Mum used to make. A crisp light pastry that melts in your mouth, tender sweet apples with a hint of spicy cloves. And, if you use organically grown apples, you can help to look after our environment.

Calories per portion: 226   **SERVES 6**

10 oz/300 g plain flour
pinch of salt
2½ oz/65 g white vegetable fat
2½ oz/65 g margarine
1½ lb/675 g cooking apples
juice of ½ lemon
6-10 cloves
3 oz/75 g golden
   granulated sugar
2 tsp caster sugar

Preheat oven to Gas 6, 400°F, 200°C. Sieve the flour into a large mixing bowl and add the salt. Cut the white fat and margarine into small pieces then add to the flour. Rub the ingredients together, using your fingers until the mixture resembles fine breadcrumbs. Mix to a soft and pliable, but not sticky, dough with 5 tbsp cold water. Turn out on to a lightly floured surface and knead until smooth and free from cracks. Wrap, then chill in the fridge for 20-30 mins. (By allowing the pastry to relax it has less of a tendency to shrink away from the sides of the dish.)

Remove from the fridge. Cut pastry in half. Roll out one half on a lightly floured surface and use to line a 9 in × 1½ in/23 cm × 4 cm deep glass pie dish. Ease pastry carefully around sides of dish and allow to come up about ¼ in/6 mm over outside edge. Trim neatly. Roll out remaining pastry for lid. Any extra pastry can be used for decoration.

Wash and dry the apples, peel then core. Cut into ¼ in/6 mm slices and leave immersed in a bowl of water to which you've added the juice of ½ lemon (the lemon juice will help prevent the apples turning brown). Drain, then arrange the apple slices in pastry-lined dish. Sprinkle with the cloves and granulated sugar.

Dampen edges of pastry with cold water then carefully lift pastry lid on top, ensuring that you don't stretch the pastry otherwise it will shrink during cooking. Trim and seal edges firmly together. Make a decorative edge by using your thumb or forefingers.

Brush the top of the pie lightly with a little water and make a hole in the centre to allow the steam to escape. Roll out the leftover pastry trimmings and cut into leaf shapes and place on top of pie. Sprinkle lightly with the caster sugar.

Bake in the oven for 20 mins, then reduce oven temperature to Gas 4, 350°F, 180°C, and continue to bake for 15-20 mins or until the filling is cooked and the pastry is golden brown.

This is delicious served hot with custard or with cream when cool.

HANDY TIPS

If you fancy a change use some other flavourings instead of the cloves. Try 1½ tsp cinnamon powder, or grated rind of a lemon or a small orange. Or you can add 2 oz/50 g sultanas or even mixed peel. They're all delicious!

1. Assemble ingredients for pastry, then sieve flour into a large mixing bowl

2. Cut fat into pieces and rub into flour until mixture resembles breadcrumbs

3. Peel cooking apples, core then cut into ¼ in/6 mm slices. Leave in water

4. Arrange apples in pastry-lined dish, add sugar and cloves, cover with pastry lid

5. Brush edges of pastry, seal firmly then pinch around edge with thumbs

6. Brush top with water, make a small hole in top, decorate with leaves

SPOTTED DICK

Everybody's favourite steamed pud – full of currants and with a hint of lemon. It's so deliciously light, and served with custard or a tangy lemon sauce, the whole family won't be able to stop eating this pud until every last mouthful has gone.

3 oz/75 g self-raising flour

4 oz/100 g fresh white
   breadcrumbs

3 oz/75 g shredded suet or
   vegetable suet

2 oz/50 g granulated sugar

6 oz/175 g currants

grated rind 1 lemon

5-7 tbsp milk

FOR THE LEMON SAUCE:

2 lemons, scrubbed

1 level tbsp cornflour

3-4 tbsp caster sugar

½ oz/15 g butter

Sift flour into a large mixing bowl. Add the breadcrumbs, suet, sugar, currants and lemon rind. Stir until thoroughly mixed. Gradually add the milk and mix to a soft, but not sticky, dough. Turn out on to a lightly floured surface and knead until smooth. Shape into a roll about 8 in/20.5 cm in length and 3 in/7.5 cm thick.

Pleat together one sheet of lightly greased greaseproof paper and one sheet of tin foil. Fold over loosely to encase the roll completely, but leave room for expansion.

Alternatively, place the pudding in a clean tea towel or pudding cloth. Tie the ends securely with string.

Place in top of a steamer and steam the pudding for 2½-3 hrs over a pan of simmering water.

Or you can place the foil-wrapped pudding in a roasting tin half filled with boiling water. Cook in a preheated oven, Gas 4, 350°F, 180°C, for 1½-2 hrs. Ensure that the water level remains constant throughout cooking.

Remove from the steamer or roasting tin and leave for 5 mins on a wire cooling rack to allow the excess moisture to drain off. Remove from cloth and serve with custard or a delicious lemon sauce.

To make the sauce, grate the rind from the lemons, squeeze out juice and make up to ½ pint/300 ml with water. Place rind and juice in a small pan and bring to the boil.

Blend the cornflour with a little water then stir into the boiling liquid. Continue to cook for 2-3 mins, stirring throughout until the sauce thickens and coats the back of a wooden spoon.

Remove from the heat, stir in sugar to taste and the butter. Continue stirring until the sugar has dissolved and the butter has melted.

HANDY TIP

The spotted dick can be microwaved, but will need eating immediately. Wrap loosely in greaseproof paper. Cook on High for 7-8 mins, then leave to stand for 2 mins. Serve immediately.

1. Sift flour into large mixing bowl. Add breadcrumbs, suet, sugar and currants

2. Scrub lemons dry, grate rind into bowl; use pastry brush to remove rind

3. Mix ingredients thoroughly, then mix to a soft but not sticky dough with the milk

4. Sprinkle surface with flour; shape into an 8 in/20.5 cm roll, 3 in/7.5 cm thick

5. Place roll in a piece of greaseproof paper, then tinfoil, and fold over loosely

6. Tie ends, put in steamer; place over steaming water and steam for 2½ -3 hrs

THE PERFECT PANCAKE

No more pulling it off the ceiling or scraping it from the bottom of the pan with this easy to follow, perfect pancake guide. This is an ideal recipe for serving on Shrove Tuesday – or any day of the year.

Calories per portion: 286

SERVES 4

4 oz/100 g plain flour
pinch of salt
1 egg, size 3, beaten
½ pint/300 ml milk
1 oz/25 g melted butter, cooled
½-1 oz/15-25 g white vegetable
   fat or 1-2 tbsp oil for frying
FOR THE SAUCE:
1 orange
1 lemon
4 oz/100 g lump sugar

Sift the flour and salt into a mixing bowl, make a well in the centre and then add the egg. Gradually mix in the milk, drawing in the flour from the sides of the bowl until a smooth batter is formed. Beat well then leave to stand for 30 mins. Stir in the cooled butter.

Heat ½ oz/15 g of fat or 1 tbsp oil in a 7 in/18 cm frying pan. When hot, pour off and reserve for regreasing the pan as necessary. Pour in 3 tbsp batter, tilting the pan slightly so the base is evenly coated. Cook over a moderate heat until golden brown, toss or flip the pancake over then cook on the other side for a further 2 mins or until golden.

Repeat, lightly greasing the pan until all the batter has been used. Keep the pancakes warm by placing on a plate over a pan of gently simmering water with a sheet of greaseproof paper between each one.

Cooked pancakes can be kept for up to one week in the fridge, interleaved with sheets of greaseproof paper. Reheat either by placing in the oven at Gas 5, 375°F, 190°C, for 20 mins or by frying in a lightly greased frying pan for 2-3 mins on each side.

To make the sauce, remove peel from half the orange and half the lemon with a zester or cut into very thin strips with a sharp knife. Then squeeze the juice from both halves and make up to ½ pint/300 ml with cold water.

Cut the remaining orange and lemon into thin slices and reserve for decoration. Put the fruit juice mixed with water and sugar in a heavy-based pan with the fruit peel, then place over a gentle heat and stir until dissolved.

Bring to the boil and boil for 5-7 mins or until a light syrup is formed.

To serve: place two pancakes on each warmed serving plate, pour a little sauce over and decorate with orange and lemon slices. Serve the remaining sauce separately.

HANDY TIP

For apple pancakes, make the plain pancakes as before and keep warm.
Mix 3 oz/75 g sultanas with the contents of a 14 oz/397 g can of stewed apples and 1-2 tsp ground cinnamon. Fill the pancakes and serve sprinkled with a little caster sugar and the cinnamon.

1. Assemble and weigh your ingredients – for both the pancakes and sauce

2. Make a well in the centre of the flour and then pour in the beaten egg

3. Pour about 3 tbsp of batter into the pan, tilting it from side to side

4. Cook over a moderate heat then toss
or flip the pancake to cook other side

5. Remove the peel from half the orange
and lemon with knife or zester

6. Simmer the fruit juice with water
and lump sugar, stirring until dissolved

TREACLE PUDDING

Go on, tempt them with their favourite pud, they just won't be able to resist this delicious light sponge, oozing with a mouthwatering golden syrup. This great recipe is sure to impress and is guaranteed to satisfy the heartiest of appetites.

Calories per portion: 403   **SERVES 6**

- 9 tbsp golden syrup
- 6 oz/175 g butter or margarine
- 6 oz/175 g caster sugar
- 2 eggs, size 3
- 2 egg whites, size 3
- 8 oz/225 g self-raising flour, sifted
- 1 tbsp skimmed milk
- 1 large lemon, scrubbed
- 2 tbsp cornflour

Grease a 2½ pint/1.5 litre pudding basin, then line the base with a small round of greased greaseproof paper.

Spoon 3 tbsp of the golden syrup into the bottom of the basin. Cream together the fat and sugar until light and fluffy. Beat together the whole eggs and the egg whites, then gradually beat them into the creamed mixture, beating well between each addition. (If the mixture starts to curdle, beat in 1 or 2 tbsp of the self-raising flour.) Carefully fold in the flour with a metal spoon. Add enough milk to give a soft dropping consistency. Spoon mixture into the pudding basin, on top of the syrup.

Cover basin with a large sheet of lightly greased foil, pleated in the

middle to allow for expansion, and making sure that the foil is tightly tucked under the rim of the basin. Fold a long piece of foil, about 24 in/51 cm long, lengthways four times to form a sling. Put the basin in the centre of the foil sling, then carefully lower it into a large saucepan.

Pour in boiling water until it comes halfway up the side of the basin. Cover the saucepan with a tightly fitting lid and cook the pudding on a low heat for 2½ hrs, replenishing the water from time to time.

About 15 mins before serving the pudding, remove the rind from the lemon with a lemon zester, or a grater, and put into a small saucepan with the remaining golden syrup and the strained juice of the lemon made up to ½ pint/300 ml with cold water. Stir over heat until the syrup melts and blends smoothly with the lemon juice.

Blend cornflour with 2 tbsp water. Stir into sauce, boil gently until thick. Pour into a serving jug, keep warm.

To unmould pudding, use the foil sling to remove the basin from the saucepan and remove the foil from the top. Place a large plate on top of the basin, then invert the basin and plate together. Carefully lift the basin, wearing oven gloves for protection. Remove the small round of greaseproof paper from top of pudding.

Serve hot with lemon and syrup, and/or custard. A little extra syrup may be spooned on top of the pudding after turning out if desired.

1. Beat margarine and sugar together until the mixture is pale and fluffy

2. Gradually add the beaten eggs, beating well between each addition

3. Sift in the self-raising flour, then fold in carefully with a metal spoon

4. Put syrup in bottom of greased basin, then spoon sponge mixture on top

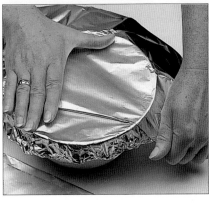

5. Cover basin tightly with a foil sheet, pleated to allow for expansion

6. Using oven gloves for protection, turn pudding out on to a warmed plate

BREAD PUDDING

A pinch of spice with a hint of orange, full of plump, sweet raisins, sultanas and currants, this pud is really easy to make. Serve it hot with custard or cold as a mid-morning break – it's sure to be an all-time family favourite.

Calories per portion: 347   **SERVES 10**

1 stale, large white sliced loaf, crusts removed

½ pint/300 ml milk

2 oz/50 g vegetable suet

2 oz/50 g demerara sugar

4 oz/100 g raisins

4 oz/100 g sultanas

3 oz/75 g currants

1½ tsp mixed spice

grated rind of 1 orange

1 egg, size 3

2 tsp granulated sugar

Preheat oven to Gas 4, 350°F, 180°C. Lightly grease a 6 in × 10 in/15 cm × 26 cm ovenproof dish with a little oil. If liked, you can use a small roasting tin or oblong cake tin.

Cut the bread into small squares and place in a large mixing bowl. Pour the milk over and leave covered for at least 30 mins. The milk needs to have been completely absorbed and the bread very soft. Beat the bread with a wooden spoon until smooth and free from lumps. You must ensure that all the lumps are removed otherwise after the pudding is cooked you will find large pieces of bread that are very solid and unpalatable.

Add the suet, then demerara sugar to the bread and mix well. Beat in the raisins, sultanas and currants. Add the mixed spice. If you like a really spicy pudding add another teaspoon of mixed spice, then add the grated orange rind. Lightly beat the egg, then beat into the mixture. Beat well with a wooden spoon to ensure that all the ingredients are thoroughly incorporated. Spoon into the prepared dish and smooth over the top.

Bake on the centre shelf of the oven for 1¼ - 1½ hrs or until the pudding is cooked. It should feel firm to the touch and the top should be golden brown. Remove from the oven and sprinkle with the granulated sugar.

If serving hot, cut into squares and serve with freshly made custard. If serving cold, mark into squares and leave in the dish until cool before cutting through and removing from the dish. Store in an airtight tin or wrapped in tin foil. It's best eaten within 2-3 days.

HANDY TIPS

If liked, you can use a brown bread (not granary) or a mixture of brown and white bread. You can also add 2 oz/50 g of chopped mixed peel when you add the dried fruit. Just reduce the quantities of the raisins and sultanas by 1 oz/25 g each.

1. Carefully trim the crusts from the sliced bread and cut into small squares

2. Place the bread into a bowl, pour the milk over and leave for 30 mins

3. Beat the soaked bread with a wooden spoon until it is smooth

4. Add the demerara sugar to the bread, then add the dried fruit

5. After adding the dried fruit, add the spice and the beaten egg

6. Spoon the mixture into a lightly greased dish and smooth the top

SUSSEX POND PUDDING

An old-fashioned recipe originating from the South of England, this pudding gets its name as during cooking the lemon bursts and combines with the butter and sugar, making a delicious sauce.

Calories per portion: 581

SERVES 6

10 oz/300 g self-raising flour

pinch of salt

5 oz/150 g shredded suet

4 oz/100 g soft brown sugar

4 oz/100 g butter

1 large lemon or 2 small lemons,
preferably unwaxed

custard to serve

Sieve the flour and salt into a mixing bowl then stir in the suet. Mix with approximately 8 fl oz/250 ml cold water to form a soft but not sticky dough. Turn out on to a lightly floured surface and knead until smooth. Reserve one third of the pastry for lid, then roll out the remainder to a 14 in/35 cm circle.

Lightly grease a 2½ pint/1.5 litre basin and line with the rolled-out pastry, easing the pastry with the fingertips to ensure a smooth, even fit. Trim the edge neatly with a round-bladed knife.

Place half the sugar in the basin, top with half the butter, cut into small cubes. Scrub and dry the lemon then prick all over with a skewer or point of a sharp knife. (This will ensure that the lemon softens and bursts and you will achieve the delicious pond of sauce in the finished pudding.) Sprinkle the remaining sugar over and add the rest of the butter, cut into small cubes.

Roll out the reserved pastry into a circle for the lid. Dampen edge of the pastry in the basin then place lid in position. Trim neatly then seal edges firmly. Cover with a double sheet of aluminium foil, pleated in the centre to allow for expansion. You can use a pudding cloth if preferred. Place basin on a double strip of foil (to enable you to lift the pudding out of the steamer easily). Place in a steamer.

Bring a pan of water to the boil, place the steamer on top. Steam steadily for 4 hrs, replenishing as necessary with boiling water. The water in the pan should be at least halfway up the sides.

When cooked, serve pudding straight from the basin, so everyone gets a portion of lemon and toffee-flavoured sauce. Serve with custard.

HANDY TIP

Use one large orange instead of the lemon in the filling.

1. Place sieved flour and salt into bowl, add suet. Mix to a soft dough with water

2. Reserve one third of pastry. Roll out remainder and use to line the basin

3. Trim round the pastry edge neatly. Prick lemon all over with a skewer

4. Add half the sugar and butter, cut into cubes, then place lemon on top

5. Add remaining sugar and butter. Roll reserved pastry into a circle for lid

6. Cover pudding with a double sheet of aluminium foil, pleated in the centre

PROFITEROLES

Deliciously crispy small choux buns,
filled with lightly whipped cream and
topped with a rich, velvety smooth
chocolate sauce... just heavenly. No-one
will be able to resist this special dessert!

3½ oz/90 g unsalted butter
5 oz/150 g plain flour
pinch of salt
4 eggs, beaten, size 3
½ pint/300 ml whipping cream
FOR THE CHOCOLATE SAUCE:
8 oz/225 g plain chocolate
3 oz/75 g unsalted butter
4 tbsp milk

Preheat oven to Gas 6, 400°F, 200°C. Melt the butter in a small pan with ½ pint/300 ml water. Bring to the boil, then remove from heat and add all the flour and salt. Beat with a wooden spoon until all the flour has been incorporated and the mixture forms a ball in the centre of the pan. Cool slightly, then gradually add the eggs a little at a time, beating well between each addition.

Place the mixture in a piping bag fitted with a 1½ in/4 cm plain piping nozzle, and pipe about 16-20 small buns on to a dampened baking sheet – leave a little space between each bun to allow for expansion.

Bake on the shelf above centre of oven for 15-20 mins or until well risen and golden brown. Remove from the oven and, with a sharp knife, make a small slit in the side of each bun. Return to the oven for 3-5 mins to allow the buns to dry out. Transfer to a wire cooling rack and leave until cold.

Whip the cream until thick, then place in a piping bag fitted with the

small plain nozzle, and fill each bun with the cream. Place on the serving dish, to form a pyramid.

Break the chocolate into small pieces, place in a bowl with the butter, and melt over a pan of gently simmering water. Stir with a wooden spoon until smooth, glossy and free from lumps. Remove the bowl from the pan and gradually beat in the milk. Continue to beat until the chocolate sauce is completely smooth and glossy. Pour attractively over the choux buns and serve immediately.

HANDY TIPS

If liked, flavour the whipped cream with a little Tia Maria to taste. You can also use real chocolate or vanilla soft scoop ice-cream, instead of the cream, to fill the choux buns.

1. Gently melt the butter in the water in a small pan, then bring to the boil

2. Add the flour and salt all at once and beat well with a wooden spoon

3. Beat thoroughly until mixture is smooth and glossy and forms a ball in pan

4. Add the beaten eggs a little at a time, beating well between each addition

5. Using a piping bag with a plain nozzle, pipe small buns on to a baking sheet

6. Fill the cooled profiteroles with the whipped cream just before serving

CHOCOLATE ROULADE

Why don't you spoil all the family with this wickedly delicious dessert? It's full of velvety smooth chocolate, sweet juicy satsumas and lashings of whipped cream.

Calories per portion: 490   **SERVES 8**

6 oz/175 g plain chocolate

4 tbsp brandy, rum or fruit juice

8 oz/225 g caster sugar

5 eggs, size 3, separated

2 tbsp icing sugar, sieved

¾ pint/450 ml whipping cream

7½ oz/220 g can satsuma segments in natural juice

1 satsuma, peeled and segmented

2 limequats or 1 lime

Preheat oven to Gas 4, 350°F, 180°C. Lightly grease a 12 in x 9 in/30 cm x 23 cm Swiss roll tin. Line the base and sides with one complete sheet of greased greaseproof paper. The paper needs to stand at least 2 in/5 cm above the sides of the tin.

Break chocolate into pieces and place in a small heatproof bowl with the brandy, rum or fruit juice. Place over a pan of gently simmering water and stir until the chocolate has melted. Beat lightly until smooth and free from lumps. Allow to cool.

In a large bowl, add the sugar to the egg yolks and beat with a wooden spoon until thick, creamy and doubled in volume. Beat in the cooled chocolate and mix well.

Whisk the egg whites until stiff and standing in peaks. Carefully fold into the chocolate mixture in a figure of eight movement. Be careful not to over mix but do ensure the egg white is completely incorporated. Pour into the prepared tin, tap lightly to remove any air bubbles and so that mixture is spread evenly in the tin.

Bake on shelf above the centre for 20-25 mins, or until the top is set and a crust has formed. Remove from oven. Cover the surface with a sheet of damp greaseproof paper and a damp clean tea towel. Leave overnight or for at least 8 hrs.

Next day sprinkle a large sheet of greaseproof paper with the icing sugar. Turn the roulade out on to the paper and carefully discard the lining paper.

Whip the cream until thick, then spread one third of the cream over the roulade to within ¼ in/6 mm of the edge. Drain the satsumas and dry on absorbent kitchen paper, then arrange over the cream leaving a gap at the bottom, top and sides. Holding the greaseproof paper with one hand, carefully roll up the roulade.

Place the roulade on a serving platter, then cover completely with the remaining cream. Mark the top and sides with a fork. Arrange the fresh satsuma segments along the bottom edges of the dish. Cut the limequats into thin slices or the lime into quarters and arrange on top of the cream.

HANDY TIP

You must use a sheet of greaseproof paper when lining the tin or the roulade will break in the middle when rolling up.

1. Break chocolate into pieces, place in bowl with brandy, rum or juice. Melt

2. Beat the cooled chocolate into the egg mixture until thoroughly mixed

3. Fold whisked egg whites into the chocolate mixture using a spatula

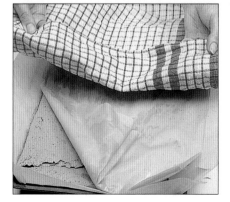
4. Cover cooked roulade with damp greaseproof paper and a damp tea towel

5. Arrange satsumas over cream leaving a gap at bottom, top and sides

6. Holding the greaseproof paper with one hand, gently roll up the roulade

CHOCOLATE PEAR PUD

This rich, moist chocolate upside-down sponge is topped with juicy slices of caramelized pears. It is delicious served hot or cold with lightly whipped cream or a smooth creamy chocolate custard sauce.

Calories per portion: 718   **SERVES 6**

2 large firm pears, such
  as comice
2 oz/50 g caster sugar
¼ pint/150 ml dry white
  wine, optional
½ lemon
3 oz/75 g butter or margarine
3 oz/75 g demerara sugar
FOR THE CHOCOLATE FILLING:
6 oz/175 g butter or margarine
6 oz/175 g caster sugar
3 eggs, size 3, beaten
5 oz/150 g self-raising
  flour, sieved
2 oz/50 g ground almonds
1 oz/25 g cocoa powder

Preheat oven to Gas 4, 350°F, 180°C. Peel the pears, taking care to remove any bruised parts, cut in half and carefully scoop out the core using a teaspoon.

Dissolve the 2 oz/50 g caster sugar in a large frying pan with the wine, if using and ½ pint/300 ml water. If you are not using the wine, use ¾ pint/450 ml of water. Squeeze the juice from the lemon half, and add to the pan with a few strips of lemon rind. Add the pears then poach gently, turning at least once during cooking, to help keep their colour. Cook for 5-8 mins (the time will depend on how ripe the pears were initially). Drain and allow them to cool. Cut the pears into thin slices, cover half and reserve.

Beat the 3 oz/75 g butter or margarine and demerara sugar until creamy then spread over the base of an 8 in/20.5 cm round cake tin. Arrange half the pear slices in a spiral over the butter mixture (if preferred you can use all the pear slices at this stage).

Cream the 6 oz/175 g butter or margarine with the caster sugar until light and fluffy, then gradually beat in the eggs with a little of the sieved flour between each addition. Fold in the remaining flour with the ground almonds. Sift cocoa powder into the mixture and fold in with 2-3 tbsp cooled boiled water to form smooth dropping consistency. Spoon over pears in tin and smooth top with a palette knife.

Bake on the centre shelf for 35-45 mins or until cooked. The sponge should spring back when lightly touched with the finger. Remove from the oven and leave for 5 mins.

Lightly run a round-bladed knife around the edge of the cake tin then invert on to a serving plate. Remove the tin then decorate with the reserved pear slices by carefully inserting them in between the cooked slices.

HANDY TIP

Use drained canned satsumas or pineapple slices for a change.

1. Peel two large pears then cut in half and carefully core using a teaspoon

2. Poach halved pears in a large frying pan with a few strips of lemon rind

3. Cream butter or margarine with the demerara. Carefully spread over tin base

4. Thinly slice the drained, cooled pear halves. Arrange over butter mixture

5. Cream fat and sugar, beat in eggs, flour and almonds. Sift in cocoa powder

6. Carefully spoon chocolate mixture over pears. Smooth top with a palette knife

CHOCOLATE SOUFFLE

Don't think you can't make a perfect soufflé – it's so much easier than you'd imagine. Just follow this step-by-step guide, and you'll have delicious results every time. So treat everyone to the lightest chocolate pud ever.

Calories per portion: 509　　　　　　**SERVES 4**

4 oz/100 g plain chocolate
3 tbsp brandy, rum or water
¾ pint/450 ml milk
2 oz/50 g caster sugar
1½ oz/40 g plain flour
1 oz/25 g butter
4 eggs, size 3

Preheat oven to Gas 4, 350°F, 180°C. Lightly butter a 7 in × 3 in/18 cm × 7.5 cm deep soufflé dish. Place a baking sheet in the oven 10 mins before baking the soufflé – this will help the soufflé to rise.

Break the chocolate into small pieces and put into a bowl. Add the brandy, rum or water and place over a saucepan of gently simmering water. Stir until chocolate has completely melted and is smooth.

Heat all but 4 tbsp of the milk to blood heat then gradually stir the warmed milk into the melted chocolate. Stir in the sugar. Blend the flour with the reserved milk to make a smooth paste. Using a balloon whisk, gradually whisk the flour paste into the chocolate mixture.

Pour mixture into a clean saucepan, place over a gentle heat and stir continuously until thickened and smooth. Cook for a further minute. Add butter, stirring gently throughout until it has been thoroughly incorporated. Remove from the heat and allow mixture to cool slightly.

Separate the eggs and place the egg whites into a large clean bowl. Add the yolks one at a time to the cooled chocolate mixture beating well after each addition. Whisk the whites until stiff and standing in peaks. Carefully fold into the mixture using a spatula or metal spoon. Take care not to over mix otherwise you will remove the air you have whisked in.

Turn the mixture into the prepared soufflé dish and place on the preheated baking sheet. Bake for 35-45 mins or until well risen and firm to the touch. Serve the soufflé immediately with cream or fromage frais.

HANDY TIP

This pudding, if liked, can be prepared up to the stage before whisking the egg whites. When ready to cook the soufflé whisk the egg whites until stiff, fold into the cold chocolate mixture, turn into the prepared dish and cook as before.
Do not keep opening the oven door during cooking as this can cause soufflés to sink.
For a hot mocha soufflé, substitute 3 tbsp of strong black coffee for the brandy, rum or water, then proceed as before.

1. Melt the chocolate pieces in bowl over pan of gently simmering water

2. Gradually stir in the warmed milk, beating well after each addition

3. Blend flour to a smooth paste with the reserved milk, whisk into mixture

4. In a clean pan, gently heat chocolate mixture until thick, add butter

5. Cool slightly, add yolks one at a time. Beat well after each addition

6. Whisk egg whites until stiff, then gradually fold into the mixture

CHOCOLATE PIE

A rich, crumbly pastry filled with a mouth-watering chocolate mousse, makes this pie a dessert that will really impress. This recipe tastes and looks delicious. No one will ever guess just how easy it is to make.

Calories per portion: 402 **SERVES 12**

FOR THE PASTRY:
7 oz/200 g plain flour
5 oz/150 g soft margarine
1 orange
3 oz/75 g ground almonds
2 oz/50 g caster sugar
1 egg, size 3
FOR THE FILLING:
8 oz/225 g plain chocolate
grated rind of 1 orange
3-4 tbsp Cointreau
6 eggs, size 5, separated
1 oz/25 g gelatine
¼ pint/150 ml whipping cream, whipped

Preheat oven to Gas 6, 400°F, 200°C. Sift flour into large mixing bowl and add the margarine in one whole piece. Scrub the orange and dry well, then finely grate rind and add to bowl. Stir in the ground almonds and sugar. Add the egg, then, using your hands, bind together with approx 1 tbsp of cold water. Knead until smooth, wrap in clearwrap then chill in fridge for 30 mins.

Knead lightly then roll out on a lightly floured surface and use to line a

12 in/30 cm loose-bottomed fluted flan tin. Carefully ease the pastry into the fluted sides and the base, taking care not to break or tear the pastry. Roll the rolling pin across the top to give a clean edge.

Place a sheet of greaseproof paper and baking beans in the flan, or a sheet of foil shaped to fit the base, then bake blind in oven for 15 mins, or until it's cooked. Remove the greaseproof paper and baking beans or tin foil for the last 5 mins of cooking time. Remove pastry case from oven and leave until cold.

To make the filling, break the chocolate into small pieces, then place in a bowl over a pan of gently simmering water. Add the grated orange rind and the Cointreau. Allow chocolate to melt, stirring occasionally. Remove from the heat and beat until smooth. Leave to cool for 5 mins.

Separate eggs then beat yolks into cooled chocolate, one at a time, beating well between each addition.

Melt the gelatine in 4 tbsp of very hot water, cool slightly then pour in a thin steady stream into the mixture, stirring throughout.

Whisk the egg whites until stiff and standing in soft peaks. Carefully fold into the chocolate mixture, ensuring that the egg whites are thoroughly incorporated. Pour the mixture into the cold baked flan case and leave in the fridge for at least 2 hrs. Whip the cream until thick then place in a piping bag fitted with a large star nozzle and decorate the top of the pie.

1. Sift flour into a mixing bowl, add margarine then the grated orange rind

2. Roll the pastry out on a floured surface and use to line a 12 in/30 cm flan tin

3. Place chocolate and rind in a bowl over a pan of simmering water. Add Cointreau

4. Stir chocolate until smooth, cool slightly, beat in egg yolks one at a time

5. Whisk egg whites until stiff then carefully fold into the chocolate mixture

6. Pour mousse into the pastry case. Leave for at least 2 hrs before decorating

CHOCOLATE CHEESECAKE

Make the richest, delicious cheesecake ever! With a crisp chocolatey biscuit base, a tangy orange and creamy chocolate cheese filling and just a little more chocolate to top it off.

Calories per portion: 396　　　　　　　**CUTS INTO 12 SLICES**

FOR THE BASE:
2½ oz/65 g unsalted butter
4 oz/100 g plain chocolate
8 oz/225 g digestive biscuits
FOR THE FILLING:
3 eggs, size 5, separated
3 oz/75 g caster sugar
grated rind and juice of
**　1 large orange**
1 lb/450 g low-fat cream cheese
4 oz/100 g plain chocolate
2 tbsp brandy
1 oz/25 g gelatine
¼ pint/150 ml double cream
chocolate curls and icing sugar
**　to decorate**

Lightly butter sides and base of an 8 in/20.5 cm loose-bottomed cake tin. To make base, place butter and chocolate in a heavy-based pan over a gentle heat and allow chocolate to melt, stirring occasionally.

Draw the pan to one side and sir until smooth and free from lumps. Place the biscuits in a polythene bag and, using a rolling pin, crush finely. Stir the biscuits into the melted chocolate, then mix well. Spoon into the buttered tin and, using the back of a spoon, press into the base and sides. Chill.

Place the egg yolks and caster sugar in a bowl and whisk until thick and creamy, then whisk in the orange rind and juice. Add the cream cheese to the mixture, then whisk again until thoroughly mixed. Melt the chocolate and brandy together in a bowl over a pan of gently simmering water, stir well, until smooth, leave to one side.

Dissolve gelatine in 4 tbsp hot water, allow to cool slightly. Whisk reserved egg whites until standing in peaks. Whip cream until softly peaking.

Once the gelatine has cooled, pour into the cream cheese mixture in a thin, steady stream. Fold in the cream, then the egg whites. Mix lightly together until all ingredients are incorporated.

Divide the mixture in half, then stir the melted plain chocolate into one half and mix lightly together. Spoon the two mixtures alternately into the prepared cheesecake base and carefully smooth over the top. Leave to set in the fridge for at least 4 hrs.

When ready to serve, remove the cheesecake from the tin and place on serving plate. Arrange chocolate curls on top, then dust with sieved icing sugar. Serve with fruit.

HANDY TIP

Try adding 3 oz/75 g chopped toasted shelled hazelnuts to the chocolate mixture for an added crunch!

1. Melt butter and chocolate in a pan. Add finely crushed biscuits and mix well

2. Using the back of a spoon, press biscuit mixture into base and sides of tin

3. Whisk egg yolks and caster sugar together, whisk in orange rind and juice

*4. After adding the cream cheese, stir
in the gelatine in a thin steady stream*

*5. Divide the mixture in half, then fold
one half into the melted chocolate*

*6. Spoon the two mixtures alternately into
the chilled biscuit case and smooth top*

CHOCOLATE TOFFEE PUD

Lashings of delicious toffee sauce poured over a steaming hot chocolate pudding makes this a treat no one can resist. Follow this easy step-by-step guide to enjoy a perfect pudding every time.

Calories per portion: 764

SERVES 6

3 oz/75 g plain chocolate, broken into squares

6 oz/175 g butter

6 oz/175 g caster sugar

3 eggs, size 3, beaten

2 tbsp milk

¼ tsp vanilla essence

5½ oz/165 g self-raising flour

½ oz/15 g cocoa

FOR THE SAUCE:

2 oz/50 g soft brown sugar

2 oz/50 g butter

¼ pint/150 ml double cream

1 tsp lemon juice

1 tsp arrowroot

Grease a 2 pint/1.2 litre pudding basin with a little butter or oil. Place the chocolate in a small bowl and place over a pan of simmering water until melted. Stir until smooth.

Cream the butter and sugar together until pale and fluffy with either a wooden spoon or an electric mixer.

Gradually add eggs to the creamed mixture, beating well between each addition. Add the milk, vanilla essence and melted chocolate and mix well to a soft consistency. Sift the flour and cocoa together and carefully fold into the chocolate mixture then spoon the mixture into the greased pudding basin.

Cut a 10 in/26 cm double circle of greaseproof paper. Make a double pleat across the centre of the paper circle and place over the basin. Using string, tie the paper securely to the basin, round the rim. Cover with a sheet of pleated foil and tie securely.

Half fill a large pan with water and bring to the boil. Place a steamer over the pan and, using a folded strip of foil to lift it, place the basin inside. Cover tightly with a lid. Steam for 2 hrs until light and well risen.

To make the sauce, place soft brown sugar and butter in a heavy-based saucepan and gently heat, stirring

occasionally until the sugar has dissolved and the butter melted. Bring to the boil without stirring until the mixture is a golden brown colour. Add the cream and lemon juice.

Place the arrowroot in a small bowl and mix with 1 tbsp water to a smooth paste. Add to the pan and heat, stirring constantly, until thickened. Remove the toffee sauce from the heat and then immediately pour it over the hot chocolate sponge. Serve at once.

HANDY TIP

Try serving the pudding with a different sauce, such as chocolate or melba.

1. Weigh out ingredients before starting to prepare the pudding

2. Melt the chocolate in small bowl over a pan of simmering water

3. Thoroughly cream the butter and sugar together until light and fluffy

4. Sift the flour and cocoa together and carefully fold into the mixture

5. Cover basin with a sheet of pleated foil and tie securely round rim

6. Place a folded strip of foil under basin to lift in and out of steamer

TARTE TATIN

This classic French dessert is a real culinary masterpiece! Crisp, light pastry is placed on top of thickly sliced, caramelized apples, then the tarte is turned upside down after cooking and sprinkled with icing sugar.

Calories per portion: 446

SERVES 8

FOR THE PATE SUCREE:
8 oz/225 g plain white flour
1½ oz/40 g caster sugar
6 oz/175 g unsalted butter
I egg yolk, size 3
FOR THE TOPPING:
4 oz/100 g vanilla or caster sugar
2 oz/50 g butter
2 lb/900 g firm dessert apples
I tsp ground cinnamon
I tsp icing sugar

Preheat the oven to Gas 7, 425°F, 220°C, 15 mins before baking.

First, make the pâte sucrée: in a large bowl, sieve flour, then stir in 1½ oz/40 g caster sugar. Either leave in the bowl or turn out on to a clean surface and form into a mound. Make a hollow in the centre, then add unsalted butter, egg yolk and 2 tsp chilled water. Using your fingertips, bring mixture together to form a soft dough. (If making pâte sucrée on a work surface, carefully draw the flour in from the sides of the mound to prevent egg and water escaping.)

Knead the dough lightly, then wrap in greaseproof paper and chill while preparing the topping.

Sprinkle 1½ tbsp vanilla or caster sugar over the base of an 8 in/20.5 cm cake tin. Melt the butter and reserve. Peel the apples, cut into quarters, then core and slice thickly. Arrange a layer of apples over the base of the cake tin in a decorative pattern. Sprinkle with half the remaining sugar, drizzle half the melted butter over, then dust lightly

with half the cinnamon. Repeat with the remaining apples, sugar, butter and cinnamon.

Place tin over a gentle heat and allow the sugar to melt, then caramelize, taking care not to burn the apples. (This process can take up to 20 mins, depending on how watery the apples are. Firm eating apples work best. You'll be able to tell when the sugar begins to caramelize as it will start to bubble up between the apples.) Remove from heat and set aside.

Meanwhile, on a lightly floured surface, roll out the chilled pâte sucrée to the size of the tin. Using the rolling-pin, carefully place the pastry over the apples and press lightly round the edge of tin.

Bake in preheated oven for 20 mins, or until pastry is cooked. If top is browning too quickly, cover with foil. Remove from the oven and invert on to a serving plate. Sprinkle the icing sugar over and serve hot or warm with the cream.

1. Form flour and sugar into mound, make a hollow, add butter and egg yolk

2. Sprinkle 1½ tbsp vanilla or caster sugar over the base of an 8 in/20.5 cm cake tin

3. Peel apples, cut into quarters, core and slice thickly, then arrange over base of tin

4. Sprinkle apples with half the remaining sugar and drizzle half melted butter over

5. Place the cake tin over gentle heat and allow the sugar to melt, then caramelize

6. On a lightly floured surface, roll out the pâte sucrée and use to cover the apples

LEMON TART

Crisp and light pastry with a subtle lemon tang, filled with a smooth lemony custard and topped with lightly caramelized lemons. This delicious tart makes an ideal dessert for a supper or lunch party. It's best served chilled so make it the day before and leave it in the fridge.

1. Place the flour into a bowl, add the fat and rub in until the mixture resembles fine breadcrumbs

2. Roll the chilled dough out on a lightly floured surface taking care not to stretch the pastry

3. Line an 8 in/20.5 cm fluted flan ring with the pastry. Roll the rolling pin across the top to ensure a neat edge

FOR THE PASTRY:

6 oz/175 g plain white flour

4 oz/100 g unsalted butter
   or margarine

1½ oz/40 g caster sugar

grated rind 1 small or
   ½ large lemon

1 egg yolk, size 3

FOR THE FILLING:

3 eggs, size 3

3 egg yolks, size 3

4 fl oz/120 ml strained
   lemon juice

2 tbsp grated lemon rind

5 oz/150 g caster sugar

1½ oz/40 g butter

3 tbsp Grand Marnier

1 lemon, sliced

cream to serve

Preheat oven to Gas 6 400°F 200°C, 15 mins before baking the pastry. To make the pastry, place the flour into a mixing bowl, rub the fat in with your fingertips until the mixture resembles fine breadcrumbs. Stir in the sugar and lemon rind. Beat the egg yolk with 4 tsp chilled water, add to the bowl then bring the mixture together to form a firm but pliable dough. Knead lightly on a floured surface until smooth, wrap in parchment or greaseproof paper then chill for 30 mins. Roll the pastry out on a lightly floured surface and use to line an 8 in/20.5 cm fluted flan ring standing on a baking sheet. Alternatively use a flan tin with a loose-bottomed base. Roll your rolling pin across the top to ensure a smooth and neat edge then place a sheet of greaseproof paper in the base and weigh down with baking beans. Chill for 20 mins then bake in the oven for 12 mins. Remove the greaseproof paper and beans then return to the oven and continue to bake for a further 5-8 mins or until the pastry case is completely cooked. Allow to become cold before filling. To prepare the filling, beat the eggs, egg yolks. lemon juice and rind with 4 oz/100 g of the caster sugar then place in a heavy-based saucepan and cook over a gentle heat. Cook stirring throughout until the mixture thickens and coats the back of a spoon. Do not allow the mixture to boil otherwise it will curdle. Remove from the heat then stir in the butter and 2 tbsp of the Grand Marnier. Stir until smooth then pour into the pastry case. Chill overnight in the fridge. Next day stir the remaining sugar in ¼ pint/150 ml of water placed in a frying pan. Place over a gentle heat and stir until the sugar has dissolved. bring to the boil then boil vigorously for 5 mins, reduce heat and add the remaining Grand Marnier. Meanwhile using a canelle knife, remove the zest from around the whole lemon in a decorative fashion, slice thinly. Place the lemon slices in the pan and poach gently for 5-8 mins turning at least once, until the lemons caramelize slightly. Remove from the pan and drain on absorbent kitchen paper. Once cold arrange on top of the tart then serve with cream.

HANDY TIP

Ring the changes and vary the flavour of the tart. Try using a mixture of oranges and lemons or use limes instead. Add 1 teaspoon of spice such as ground cinnamon or ginger to the pastry instead of the lemon rind.

4. Beat the eggs, egg yolks, sugar and lemon rind together. Gradually beat in the strained lemon juice

5. Add the butter to the thickened lemon filling then stir in 2 tbsp Grand Marnier, stir until smooth

6. Dissolve the sugar in ¼ pint./150 ml of water, add the Grand Marnier then the lemon slices and poach slices

PEAR & ALMOND TART

Crisp, almond pastry encases a mouthwatering combination of creamy custard and juicy pears in a delicious dessert. Serve with cream for an extra special family treat.

Calories per portion: 640　　　　**SERVES 6**

3 ripe pears
juice of 1 lemon
2 oz/50 g caster sugar
FOR THE PASTRY:
8 oz/225 g plain flour
¼ tsp salt
6 oz/175 g unsalted butter or
　margarine, softened slightly
2 oz/50 g ground almonds
1 oz/25 g caster sugar
1 egg, size 3, separated
FOR THE CUSTARD CREAM:
4 egg yolks, size 3
2 oz/50 g caster sugar
few drops of almond essence
1 tbsp cornflour
2 tbsp plain flour
¾ pint/450 ml milk
1 tbsp warmed apricot
　jam, sieved
toasted flaked almonds and
　lemon zest to decorate

Preheat oven to Gas 5, 375°F, 190°C, 15 mins before baking. Lightly grease a 9 in/23 cm loose-bottomed flan tin.

Core, peel and quarter pears, and sprinkle with lemon juice to avoid discolouration. Place pears in pan with

HANDY TIP

When buying pears for cooking, choose fairly firm, unblemished and even shaped fruit. Prepare and use immediately to prevent discolouration.

sugar and pour in 1 pint/600 ml water and heat until sugar is dissolved. Poach pears gently for 15 mins until tender. Allow to cool in liquid.

Meanwhile, make pastry. Sift flour and salt into a bowl and rub in fat until mixture resembles breadcrumbs. Stir in almonds and sugar and bind together with egg yolk and 2 tsp cold water to form a firm dough. Knead gently on a lightly floured surface until smooth. Wrap and chill for 30 mins.

Roll pastry out on a lightly floured surface to fit greased flan tin and gently press into tin. Using a small leaf cutter stamp out enough shapes from the trimmings to go round the pastry rim. Stick the shapes on to pastry rim with lightly beaten egg white. Prick base and chill for 30 mins. Brush all over with egg white and bake for 15-20 mins until golden. Allow to cool.

To make custard cream, whisk together egg yolks, sugar and almond essence until pale and thick, and stir in cornflour and flour. Gradually blend in the milk and place in a heatproof bowl over a pan of simmering water or a double saucepan. Stir until thickened. Cover surface of custard with greaseproof paper to prevent a skin forming and allow to cool.
Remove pastry case from tin and stand on serving board. Spoon in custard cream and smooth over top. Drain pears and arrange on top of custard. Brush with apricot jam and serve sprinkled with almonds and lemon zest, accompanied with cream.

1. Core, peel and quarter pears and sprinkle with lemon juice to avoid discolouration

2. Place pears in pan with sugar and pour in 1 pint/600 ml water. Heat until sugar is dissolved

3. Stir in almonds and sugar and bind together with egg yolk and 2 tsp water to form a firm dough

4. Using a small leaf cutter stamp out shapes from the trimmings. Stick the shapes on to pastry rim with egg white

5. Whisk together egg yolks, sugar and almond essence until pale and thick. Stir in cornflour and flour

6. Remove pastry case from tin and stand on serving board. Spoon in custard cream and smooth over top

BLACKBERRY CHARLOTTE

Make the most of the late-summer fruits and serve your family and friends a delicious taste of the country with this simply mouth-watering dessert, full of juicy blackberries and sweet apples. It's a really super treat.

Calories per portion: 464

SERVES 8

I lb/450 g blackberries, washed
  and patted dry
I lb/450 g cooking apples
finely grated rind and juice
  of I lemon
I tsp ground cinnamon
6 oz/175 g light brown sugar
4 tbsp cake crumbs
¾ large loaf white bread
4 oz/100 g butter or
  margarine, melted
I egg, size 5, beaten
I tbsp demerara sugar
a few blackberries and leaves
  to decorate

Preheat the oven to Gas 5, 375°F, 190°C. Lightly grease a 2½ pint/1.5 litre charlotte mould or a 6 in/15 cm round cake tin.

Place the blackberries in a large pan. Peel, core and thickly slice the apples and add to saucepan along with the lemon rind and juice and cinnamon. Cook gently for 10 mins until the apples have softened slightly. Stir in the brown sugar and cake crumbs.

Cut the bread into ½ in/1.25 cm thick slices and remove all the crusts. Trim two slices to fit the base of the tin and brush both sides of each slice with some melted butter or margarine. Fit into tin base. Reserve two slices for the top. Trim the remaining slices to fit the side of the tin. Dip both sides of each slice in the melted fat and arrange them closely around the side of tin, overlapping them as you go. Brush over the joins with some of the beaten egg.

Spoon in the stewed fruit and cover with the reserved slices of bread. Trim to fit and then brush the top with beaten egg. Bake for about 1 hr, or until golden brown.

Remove from the oven. Run a palette knife around the edge of the charlotte and invert on to a warmed serving plate. Sprinkle demerara sugar over the top and serve immediately, decorated with a few blackberries and leaves and accompanied by fruit-flavoured fromage frais decorated with mint.

1. Stir the light brown sugar and cake crumbs into the stewed blackberry and apple mixture

3. Dip slices in the melted fat and arrange around side of tin, overlapping as you go

5. Spoon in stewed apples and blackberries and cover with reserved slices of bread

2. Cut the ¾ loaf of white bread into ½ in/1.25 cm thick slices and remove the crusts

4. Once you have arranged the bread, brush over joins with some of the beaten egg to help seal the joins

6. Run a palette knife around edge of charlotte and invert on to a warm serving plate. Serve sprinkled with demerara sugar

ORANGE SOUFFLE

Light as a feather, this delicious dessert has a wonderfully refreshing orange flavour that will get the taste buds tingling. Follow this easy step-by-step guide and cook the best soufflé ever.

Calories per portion: 405　　　　　　　　　　　　　　　**SERVES 4**

2 large oranges

½ oz/15 g unsalted butter, melted

1½ oz/40 g butter or margarine

1½ oz/40 g plain white flour

2 oz/50 g caster sugar

2 tbsp Grand Marnier or Cointreau

4 eggs, size 3

1 tbsp icing sugar

orange zest to decorate

assorted sweet biscuits to serve

Preheat oven to Gas 4, 350°F, 180°C, 10 mins before cooking the soufflé. Place a baking sheet in the oven 5 mins before cooking the soufflé. (By placing the soufflé dish on to the hot baking sheet the heat from the baking sheet will give the soufflé an initial burst of heat thus ensuring that the soufflé rises well.)

Scrub and thoroughly dry the oranges then grate the rind finely. Add the grated rind from half an orange to the melted butter to use to brush the sides and base of a 2 pint/1.2 litre soufflé dish. Leave to one side while preparing the soufflé. Squeeze the juice from the two oranges, strain and if necessary make up to ¼ pint/150 ml with water.

Melt the 1½ oz/40 g fat in a small pan then add the flour and cook over a gentle heat for 2 mins, stirring throughout. Turn off or remove from heat, gradually stir in strained orange juice. Return the pan to the heat and cook, stirring throughout until the mixture thickens. Remove from the heat and stir in the sugar and Grand Marnier or Cointreau. Allow the mixture to cool. Separate the eggs and once the mixture has cooled, beat in the egg yolks, one at a time, beating well between each addition. Place the egg whites in a large mixing bowl. (Ensure that the bowl is completely clean, otherwise the whites will not whisk properly.) Whisk the whites until stiff and standing in soft peaks. Fold 1 tbsp of the egg white into the mixture, followed by half the remaining whites then the other half. (Take great care when folding in that you do not beat out all the air you have so carefully whisked in. Use a figure of eight movement when folding in, this ensures that the egg white is folded in evenly.)

Tap the soufflé lightly on the surface to remove any air bubbles then place on the preheated baking sheet in the oven and cook for 30-35 mins or until the soufflé is well risen and golden brown. Have ready the icing sugar in a small sieve and the orange zest.

As soon as the soufflé is cooked, remove from oven, sieve over icing sugar, decorate with zest and serve.

HANDY TIP

If liked divide the mixture between six ¼ pint/150 ml ramekin dishes, prepare as instructed then cook in the oven for 15-20 mins or until cooked. Serve at once.

1. Stir the grated rind from half an orange into the melted butter and use to brush the sides and base of dish

2. Melt the fat in a small pan then add the flour and cook over a gentle heat for 2 mins

3. Turn the heat off then gradually stir in the strained orange juice. Return to the heat and cook until thickened

4. Once the mixture has thickened, allow to cool then add the egg yolks one at a time

5. Whisk the egg whites until stiff, add 1 tbsp to the orange mixture then the remaining egg whites in two stages

6. Pour the prepared soufflé mixture into the dish and place on the preheated baking sheet and cook

APPLE STRUDEL

Deliciously light pastry filled with chunks of apple, flavoured with lemon, cinnamon and nutmeg. Don't be frightened of making strudel pastry – it's really easy, and the smell as it's cooking will start everyone's taste-buds tingling.

Calories per portion: 366   **SERVES 6**

FOR THE PASTRY:
8 oz/225 g plain flour
½ tsp salt
I egg, size 3
2 tbsp vegetable oil
FOR THE FILLING:
I lb/450 g cooking apples
I½ oz/40 g flaked almonds
2 oz/50 g seedless raisins
I tbsp grated lemon rind
½ tsp freshly grated nutmeg
½ tsp ground cinnamon
2-3 oz/50-75 g sugar
I½ oz/40 g butter, melted

Preheat oven to Gas 5, 375°F, 190°C, 10 mins before baking the strudel. Sift the flour and salt into a large mixing bowl. Make a well in the centre, add the egg with 4-5 tbsp of tepid water and the 2 tbsp oil. Mix to a pliable dough and continue to knead for about 15 mins until the dough is silky smooth and very elastic.

If liked, the dough can be made in a food mixer using the dough hook attachment – the pastry will take about 5 mins. Shape into a round ball then leave in a lightly oiled polythene bag for about I hr.

Meanwhile, prepare the filling. Peel, core and slice the apples. Place in a bowl with ½ oz/15 g of the flaked almonds, the raisins, lemon rind, nutmeg, cinnamon and sugar. Mix together lightly.

Roll the relaxed pastry out as thin as you can on a lightly floured surface with a warmed rolling pin. Then, lift the pastry up and gently stretch it from the centre towards the edge, taking care not to tear it. Cut into two 12 in x 10 in/30 cm x 26 cm oblongs and place on to individual sheets of greaseproof paper. Divide the prepared filling between each pastry oblong, brush all edges well with melted butter then carefully roll up each strudel, tucking each end into the centre and keeping the roll a neat shape.

Lift on to a greased baking sheet, with the join underneath and brush each strudel with remaining melted butter. Sprinkle with remaining almonds and bake just above the centre for 20-25 mins or until golden brown. Allow to cool slightly before dusting with a little sifted icing sugar. Serve this delicious dessert cut into slices, hot or cold with custard or cream.

HANDY TIPS

When making the strudel pastry, use a warm, flour dusted rolling pin to prevent the pastry sticking. Add the filling and roll up immediately to prevent the pastry drying out. You can use whatever sugar you prefer – caster, soft light brown or dark brown sugar, for a rich flavour.

I. Sift the flour and salt into the bowl, add the egg, then the water and oil

2. Peel and slice apple, add almonds, raisins, rind, nutmeg, cinnamon, sugar

3. Roll relaxed dough out on a lightly floured surface, using a warm rolling pin

4. Cut dough into two 12 in x 10 in/30 cm x 26 cm oblongs and arrange the filling

5. Lift greaseproof paper and carefully roll strudel, ensuring filling is encased

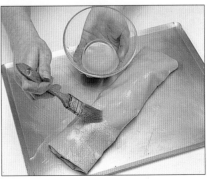

6. Place on a lightly greased baking sheet, brush with the melted butter

PEARS IN RED WINE

This classic French recipe provides a perfect ending to any meal. The pears are gently poached in a light sugar syrup with red wine, cinnamon and lemon until they are tender and have become a beautiful red colour.

Calories per portion: 162 **SERVES 6**

---

1 lemon, preferably unwaxed
6 firm pears such as William or conference – choose good even shaped pears and ones that are not damaged or bruised
6 oz/175 g caster sugar
1 cinnamon stick
8 fl oz/250 ml full-bodied red wine
cinnamon sticks and lemon peel to garnish
cream and sweet biscuits to serve

Using a vegetable peeler carefully remove a long thin strip of peel from the lemon and reserve. Cut the lemon in half and squeeze out the juice. Place the juice in a large mixing bowl and fill it with cold water. Using the vegetable peeler, peel the pears thinly but leave the stalks intact. Place the peeled pears as soon as they are peeled in the bowl of water. (The lemon juice in the water helps to ensure that the pears do not discolour before cooking.)

Place the sugar in a heavy-based pan with 6 fl oz/175 ml of water. Add the lemon peel. Lightly bash (bruise) the cinnamon stick and break in half, add to the pan. Place over a gentle heat and cook, stirring until the sugar dissolves. Bring to the boil then boil steadily for 2 mins.

Drain the pears then add to the pan, cover with a lid then poach the pears for 20-30 mins or until the pears are tender, turning the pears occasionally during cooking. (The length of time will depend on the ripeness of the pears.) Test the pears with a skewer. If the skewer is easily inserted the pears are cooked.

Once cooked add the red wine and continue to poach the pears for a further 10 mins turning them occasionally very gently with a wooden spoon. (This will allow the pears to absorb the flavour and colour of the wine.)

Carefully remove the pears from the pan and place them in a dish. Increase the heat under the pan and bring the syrup to the boil. Boil steadily

for 10 mins or until the liquid is reduced by half and has become the consistency of thick syrup. Discard the lemon rind and cinnamon stick.

If serving the pears warm, place them upright in a dish, pour over the syrup and garnish with thin strips of lemon peel and cinnamon sticks.

If serving the pears cold, pour the syrup over the pears and leave to become cold. Turn the pears frequently in the syrup. (You will get a deeper colour if the pears are served cold as they have longer sitting in the red wine syrup.) Serve pears with cream and sweet biscuits.

HANDY TIP

For a change, try using a medium dry white wine instead of the red wine, and orange peel instead of the lemon. Stir in 2 tbsp Cointreau or Grand Marnier as well for an added indulgence.

1. Using a vegetable peeler, peel the pears thinly then place in the water mixed with lemon juice

2. Place the sugar, lemon peel and cinnamon stick in a heavy-based pan with 6 fl oz/175 ml water

3. Drain the peeled pears then carefully add to the pan taking care not to damage them

4. Cover the pan with a lid then poach the pears for 20-30 mins or until tender. Test with a skewer

5. Once the pears are cooked, pour the red wine over and continue to poach for 10 mins

6. Remove the pears from the syrup then increase the heat and boil steadily until a thick syrup consistency is reached

LEMON SYLLABUB

A classic dessert that dates back to Elizabethan times, rich and creamy with a subtle tang of white wine and lemons. Simple to make, it's the perfect answer for occasions when you want a treat.

Calories per portion: Syllabub 379; Biscuits 55 **SERVES 4**

1 large lemon
¼ pint/150 ml dry white wine
3 oz/75 g caster sugar
½ pint/300 ml double cream
zested lemon rind to decorate
TUILLE BISCUITS:
2 fl oz/50 ml double cream
1 egg, size 3 separated
4½ oz/120 g icing sugar
1½ oz/40 g plain flour
½ tsp baking powder
1 oz/25 g flaked almonds

To make the syllabub, scrub the lemon and dry thoroughly then finely grate the rind and place in a bowl. Squeeze out the juice and strain into the bowl then stir in the wine. Add the sugar and stir then cover. Place in the fridge and leave to infuse for 3-4 hrs.

Add the cream to the infused liquid then gently whip together until the mixture thickens and forms soft peaks.

Spoon the mixture into four individual glass dishes and then chill for a further 3-4 hrs before serving with the tuille biscuits and decorated with zested lemon rind.

To make the tuille biscuits, preheat oven to Gas 6, 400°F, 200°C, 15 mins before baking the biscuits. Well grease 2-3 baking sheets with oil. Beat the cream and egg yolk together in a bowl until thoroughly mixed together. Sift the icing sugar then gently stir into the bowl, ensuring that there are no lumps. Sift the flour and baking powder together then add to the mixture and fold in using a metal spoon. Whisk the egg white until stiff then fold into the mixture. Place in a piping bag fitted with a small plain potato nozzle then pipe 1½ in/4 cm lengths onto the baking sheets. (Only pipe a few onto each baking sheet, as they spread.) Sprinkle the biscuits with 4-5 flaked almonds

then bake in the oven for 5-7 mins or until cooked. To tell if they are cooked, the biscuits should be completely pale golden in colour. Remove from the oven, leave for a couple of seconds then gently wrap round the handle of some clean wooden spoons. Leave for a few minutes to harden, before cooling on a wire cooling rack. This amount of mixture should make 18 biscuits. Serve with the Syllabub.

1. Scrub the lemon and dry then grate the rind finely. Place in bowl with the juice, wine and sugar

2. Pour the double cream into the chilled infused wine and lemon juice, stirring throughout

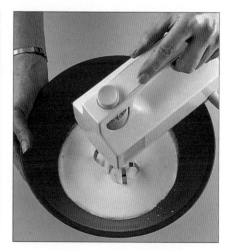

3. Gently whisk the mixture until it thickens and forms soft peaks. Spoon into glasses and chill

4. Whisk the egg white until stiff then carefully fold into the tuille mixture. Place in a piping bag

5. Pipe 1½ in/4 cm lengths onto the greased baking sheets and sprinkle with flaked almonds

6. Allow tuilles to cool for a couple of seconds. Remove from baking sheet and shape round a wooden spoon

FRUIT CRUMBLE

Make the most of fruit and cook up a scrumptious crumble. This one with apples and delicious sun-ripened apricots is an appetizing pudding for the whole family, served with custard or ice cream it's bound to be a real favourite.

Calories per portion: 550
SERVES 4

FOR THE FILLING:
2 lb/900 g cooking apples

2 cinnamon sticks

**grated rind and juice of
1 large orange**

**3-4 oz/75-100 g golden
granulated sugar**

**6 oz/175 g, no-need-to-soak
apricots**

FOR THE TOPPING:
6 oz/175 g plain flour

3 oz/75 g butter or margarine

2 tbsp bran, optional

**2 oz/50 g unrefined
granulated sugar**

Preheat oven to Gas 6, 400°F, 200°C, 15 mins before baking crumble. Peel the cooking apples and core. Slice thinly and place in a saucepan. Lightly bruise the cinnamon sticks and add to pan with the grated rind and juice of the orange and sugar to taste. Place over a gentle heat and cook for 12-15 mins or until apples are soft and pulpy. Stir the apples occasionally during cooking to prevent them burning on base of pan. Remove from heat and discard cinnamon sticks. Beat to form a purée.

Chop or snip the apricots with scissors and add to the apples. Spoon into a shallow ovenproof dish.

To make the topping: Sift the flour into a mixing bowl. Add the fat then rub in, using fingertips, until mixture resembles fine breadcrumbs. Stir in the bran if using then the sugar.

Spoon the mixture over the apple and apricots ensuring that the filling is completely covered. Press topping down lightly with the back of a spoon. Place dish on a baking sheet and bake

on the centre shelf for 30-35 mins or until topping is golden. Remove from oven and serve hot with custard or ice cream.

Variations: here are some ideas for varying the fruit filling. Add 6 oz/175 g blackberries or raspberries to the apple purée. Try stewing 1½ lb/675 g rhubarb with 1 tsp ground ginger and 2-3 tsp ginger wine with sugar to taste until soft. Or wash 1½ lb/675 g plums, cut in half and discard the stones. Simmer gently with 2-3 oz/50-75 g of sugar. Stir in 3 oz/75 g washed, dried and halved, natural coloured glacé cherries.

HANDY TIP

Make double the quantity of crumble topping. Place half in a container or polythene bag. Either freeze or store for up to one week in the fridge for a quick pudding when time is short.

1. Thinly peel the apples then carefully core, slice and place in saucepan

2. Simmer the apples with the cinnamon, sugar and the orange rind and juice

3. Beat the apples to a pulp then add the apricots — no need to soak them first

8 thin slices white bread,
    preferably one day old
4 oz/100 g redcurrants
8 oz/225 g blackcurrants
4 oz/100 g raspberries
6 oz/175 g ripe plums
4 oz/100 g strawberries
6 oz/175 g cooking apples
4 oz/100 g caster sugar
fresh mint leaves to decorate
fresh cream to serve

Place the thinly-sliced bread on a chopping board, trim off the crusts and discard them. Reserve 2 of the slices and use the remainder to line the base and sides of a 1½ pint/900 ml pudding basin. Ensure that there are no gaps in the bread.

Wash and dry the red and blackcurrants lightly, discarding any leaves or under-ripe fruit, then prepare the currants by stripping them off the stalks. Place them in a saucepan with the raspberries. Reserve a few currants to decorate. Wash the plums, cut in half and discard the stone, chop roughly and add to the pan. Hull the strawberries, wash lightly, then chop roughly and add to pan. Peel the cooking apples, and discard the cores, chop roughly and add to pan with the sugar and 2 tbsp of cold water.

Bring slowly to the boil, lower the heat, and simmer very gently for 5 mins or until the fruits are soft but still retain their shape. Cool slightly for 3-4 mins then place the lightly stewed fruit into the bread-lined pudding basin. Pack down firmly with the back of a spoon or spatula, taking care not to squash the fruit too much. After filling basin to the top with fruit, carefully place reserved bread slices on top, ensuring fruit is completely covered.

Place a saucer or small plate – which will just fit inside the basin – on top of the bread, then weigh down with some heavy weights or a large, clean can. Place in the fridge, preferably overnight, to allow the juices from the fruit to soak into the bread and give the pudding its colour.

To serve, carefully invert the basin on to a flat serving plate and shake lightly to remove the basin.

Decorate the summer pudding with the reserved currants and mint leaves, and serve with cream.

HANDY TIPS

If you find that you have trouble removing the basin, carefully run a round-bladed knife between the bread and the basin to loosen the pudding. Vary the fruits according to availability and own personal tastes. For a healthier version of this pudding, try substituting brown bread for white.

1. Place the thinly sliced bread on a chopping board, trim crusts and discard

2. Line the base and sides of a 1½ pint/ 900 ml pudding basin with the bread

3. Prepare the red and blackcurrants, place in pan, then peel cooking apples

4. Place the lightly stewed fruit into the bread-lined basin, pack down firmly

5. After filling basin with the fruit, place the reserved bread slices on top

6. Place a saucer or small plate on top, then weigh down with heavy weights

HAZELNUT VACHERIN

Layers of delicious nutty meringue sandwiched together with whipped cream and fresh fruit make this scrumptious dessert. It's just ideal for those special occasions or when you simply want to give your family a super treat.

4 oz/100 g hazelnuts
4 egg whites, size 3
8 oz/225 g caster sugar
FOR THE FILLING:
½ pint/300 ml whipping cream
1-2 tbsp kirsch, optional
8 oz/225 g strawberries
8 oz/225 g raspberries

Preheat the oven to Gas 5, 375°F, 190°C, 10 mins before skinning hazelnuts. Lightly oil and line three baking sheets with vegetable parchment paper. Draw a circle in the centre of each sheet by inverting a 6 in/15 cm plate on top and tracing round it.

Skin hazelnuts, if necessary, by placing on an unlined baking sheet and baking in oven for 10 mins. Remove and cool. Rub off skins by placing in a clean tea towel and rubbing between hands. Place in a food processor or blender and blend until finely ground.

Place egg whites in a clean, grease-free glass bowl. Whisk until stiff. Add half the sugar, 1 tbsp at a time, whisking after each addition, bringing the mixture back to its original stiffness each time. Fold in remaining sugar, using a metal spoon or spatula and taking care not to over mix.

Lightly fold in the ground hazelnuts using a figure of eight movement. Place an equal amount of mixture in the centre of each drawn circle, smoothing out to the edges with a palette knife. Place in oven and bake for 15 mins. Reduce oven temperature to Gas 2, 300°F, 150°C, and continue to cook for

20-30 mins, or until meringue is firm to touch. You may need to swap the positions of the baking sheets to ensure even browning.

Remove from oven and allow to cool for at least 15 mins before transferring to wire racks. Peel off paper when cold. Whip the cream until thick, then stir in the kirsch, if using. Hull the strawberries and raspberries and rinse lightly. Leave to dry on absorbent kitchen paper. Spread cream over each meringue layer, top with fruit, then sandwich layers together. Reserve a little cream and fruit for decoration.

Place reserved cream in a piping bag fitted with a star nozzle and pipe rosettes around edge. Decorate the top with fruit, serving any remaining fruit separately.

HANDY TIPS

The meringue can be made beforehand and stored for up to two days in an airtight tin. If liked, ground almonds can be used instead of hazelnuts. Vary the fruit according to taste and availability.

1. Lightly oil and line three baking sheets, draw a circle in the centre of each

2. Whisk egg whites until stiff, whisk in half the sugar, then whisk again

3. Using a metal spoon, carefully fold in the finely ground hazelnuts

4. Place an equal amount of mixture in the centre of each drawn circle

5. Using a palette knife, spread the meringue mixture to edge of each circle

6. When cooked, remove from oven. Allow to cool, then transfer to wire racks

CREME BRULEE

Make any occasion special and cook this classic dessert. It's naughty but truly delicious, made with thick double cream and flavoured with a hint of vanilla then topped with a crunchy caramel topping. Serve with fresh fruit and sweet biscuits.

1 pint/600 ml double cream
1 tsp vanilla essence or
   1 vanilla pod
4 egg yolks, size 3
6 oz/175 g caster sugar

Preheat the oven to Gas 2, 300°F, 150°C. Pour the cream into a large mixing bowl or into the top of a double saucepan. Place over a pan of gently simmering water. Stir in the vanilla essence or add the vanilla pod. Heat through gently until almost at boiling point, then remove from heat and, if using the vanilla pod, discard.

Whisk the egg yolks with 2 oz/50 g of the sugar until doubled in size and thick and creamy. It's thick enough when the whisk leaves an impression as it's lightly drawn across the surface. Gradually whisk the warmed cream into the egg mixture, mix well.

Pour the mixture into six individual ovenproof dishes or ramekins to within ½ in/1.25 cm of the top. Place in a roasting tin then carefully pour in boiling water so that the level of the water comes halfway up the sides of the dishes.

Bake in the oven for about 1-1½ hrs, or until set. Top up the water as necessary. Take care not to allow the skin on the top of the custard to colour. When set, the top will have a slightly crusty appearance and will feel firm when pressed lightly with a finger. Remove roasting tin from the oven and take out the individual dishes. Leave until cool then refrigerate overnight.

Next day, preheat grill. Cover the custard (in each dish) with the remaining sugar, ensuring that the surface is completely covered. Tap the dishes lightly to level out the sugar.

Place under the preheated grill for 4-5 mins, or until the sugar caramelizes. Take great care at this stage not to burn the sugar. Turn the dishes to ensure even browning. Remove from grill and leave to cool, then chill.

HANDY TIPS

This dish is not suitable for freezing or cooking in a microwave. If liked, fresh fruit such as raspberries or strawberries can be placed in the dishes before pouring over the custard and baking. It can also be made in a larger ovenproof dish, such as a soufflé dish – this will then need to be cooked for at least 1½ -2 hrs.

1. Place cream in bowl over pan of simmering water, add vanilla essence

2. Cream egg yolks and sugar until thick, gradually whisk in warmed cream

3. Pour the cream mixture into six individual ovenproof or ramekin dishes

4. Place dishes in roasting tin, pour boiling water to reach halfway up sides

5. Sprinkle the brûlées with caster sugar to at least ¼ in/6 mm in depth

6. Place under a preheated grill until sugar turns to caramel. Turn occasionally

LEMON SOUFFLE

Forget what you've heard about soufflés being difficult to make – that's just a myth. As long as you follow the instructions properly, it just couldn't be easier. So don't be put off – your soufflés will be as light as a feather!

Calories per portion: 393   **SERVES 6**

finely grated rind of 3 lemons
6 tbsp lemon juice
6 eggs, size 3, separated
6 oz/175 g caster sugar
1½ tbsp gelatine
½ pint/300 ml whipping cream
1½ oz/40 g almond nibs, toasted
julienne strips of lemon to
**   decorate**

Prepare a 1½ pint/900 ml (6 in/15 cm) soufflé dish. Cut a double strip of greaseproof paper long enough to go right round the soufflé dish. Stick with tape or tie firmly in position. Ensure that the paper is at least 3 in/7.5 cm higher than the dish.

Place the lemon rind, juice, egg yolks and sugar in a large mixing bowl and place over a saucepan of gently simmering water. Whisk with an electric or balloon whisk until thick, creamy and pale in colour. The mixture should be thick enough to make a trail when the whisk is lightly pulled across the surface. Remove the bowl from the heat and continue to whisk until the mixture is cool.

Dissolve the gelatine with 3 tbsp of water in a small bowl over a pan of gently simmering water. Pour into the egg mixture in a thin steady stream. Do not add the gelatine all at once or the mixture will become lumpy with a "roping" or stringy consistency. Chill the mixture until it begins to set lightly round the outside edge.

Whip the cream until thick and standing in soft peaks. Reserve 2 tbsp for decoration. Leave covered in a small bowl in the fridge. With a metal spoon or spatula, carefully fold cream into the mixture. Whisk egg whites until stiff, but not dry, then fold into the soufflé mixture using a figure of eight movement, ensuring all the egg white is incorporated. Pour into the prepared soufflé dish. Place in fridge for at least 3 hrs or until set.

Carefully remove the greaseproof paper away from the outside of the dish. (If necessary, use a round-bladed knife to ease the paper away, in order to keep a smooth edge.) Decorate the edge of the soufflé with the toasted almonds, patting the nuts in firmly. If liked, whisk the reserved cream until stiff enough to pipe. Place the whipped cream in a piping bag fitted with a small star nozzle, then pipe small rosettes round the top edge of the soufflé and decorate with the julienne strips of lemon rind.

HANDY TIP

For a spectacular soufflé, make as instructed but replace the lemon rind and juice with orange. Place a jam jar in the centre of a glass serving bowl. Layer soufflé with grated chocolate. Remove jar when set and fill hollow with fruit.

1. Whisk egg yolks, sugar, lemon rind and juice over heat, until thick

2. Pour in the gelatine in a thin, steady stream so that there are no lumps

3. Whip cream until thick and softly peaking, fold in carefully with a spatula

4. Gently fold in the stiffly beaten egg white using a figure of eight movement

5. When firmly set, carefully ease the paper away from the soufflé dish

6. Hold soufflé with one hand, with the other carefully pat nuts round edge

MOUNT VESUVIUS

This spectacular pudding is made with delicious apricots, raspberry sorbet and vanilla ice cream, covered with super-light meringue. But what makes it really special is how you serve it – topped with lit sparklers!

Calories per portion: 527   **SERVES 8**

FOR THE SPONGE CAKE:
2 eggs, size 3
2 oz/50 g caster sugar
2 oz/50 g plain flour
FOR THE FILLING:
6 oz/175 g no-need-to-soak apricots, chopped
¼ pint/150 ml unsweetened orange juice
1¾ pint/1 litre tub vanilla ice cream
17½ fl oz/500 ml raspberry sorbet
FOR THE MERINGUE:
3 egg whites, size 3
4½ oz/120 g caster sugar
FOR THE DECORATION:
2 oz/50 g whole blanched almonds
2 tbsp demerara sugar
sparkler or dessert candle

Preheat the oven to Gas 5, 375°F, 190°C. Grease and line the base of a 7 in/18 cm sandwich tin. Whisk eggs and caster sugar until pale and thick. Sieve flour, carefully fold into egg mixture with a metal spoon, with 1 tbsp tepid boiled water. Pour into tin and bake for 20-25 mins, or until firm to the touch. Turn out on to a wire rack to cool.

To prepare filling, place apricots in pan with orange juice, bring to boil and simmer for 10 mins until soft. Leave to cool. Place the vanilla ice cream in a 2½ pint/1.5 litre pudding basin and mould up the sides using the back of a metal spoon. Freeze for approx

30 mins to harden. Mould sorbet in same way to form a layer inside ice cream. Fill centre with cooled apricots and freeze for 30 mins, or until frozen.

When ice cream is frozen, place basin in a bowl of hot water for 10 secs and loosen edges with a palette knife. Place sponge over top of dessert, turn out, then return to freezer for a further 30 mins.

Increase the oven temperature to Gas 8, 450°F, 230°C. Whisk egg whites until stiff and standing in peaks, then whisk in half the caster sugar. Whisk again until stiff, then carefully fold in remaining sugar. Place the ice cream and sponge on to a lightly greased baking sheet then spoon over the meringue, ensuring ice cream and sponge are completely covered. Press almonds into the meringue and sprinkle with the demerara sugar.

Bake in the oven for 3-4 mins or until the tips of the meringue are light brown and the meringue is set. Serve immediately with cream, decorated with a sparkler or candle, which should be removed before cutting the dessert.

HANDY TIP

Instead of using the sparkler or candle, place a metal eggcup in the top of the meringue before flash-baking. Once cooked, half fill with warmed brandy then ignite and serve.

1. Whisk the eggs and sugar in a mixing bowl until creamy, then fold in flour

2. Mould the ice cream and sorbet up the sides of a basin. Fill with apricots

3. Place the frozen dessert carefully in a bowl of hot water for 10 secs

4. Loosen with palette knife. Place sponge over dessert and turn out of basin

5. Refreeze, then place on greased baking sheet. Swirl meringue over to cover

6. Press whole almonds into meringue, sprinkle with sugar and bake

CHEESECAKE

Soft creamy cheese on a crisp, crunchy, gingery base, lightly baked then chilled, and topped with kiwi fruit and apricots that have been poached in a Grand Marnier syrup.

Calories per portion: 694   SERVES 6

8 oz/225 g gingernut biscuits

2 oz/50 g stem ginger

3 oz/75 g unsalted butter

2 lb/900 g low-fat soft
 cream cheese

6 oz/175 g caster sugar

3 eggs, size 3, beaten

1 tsp vanilla essence

8 oz/225 g fresh apricots

2 oz/50 g sugar

2 tbsp Grand Marnier

2 kiwi fruit, peeled and
 thinly sliced

Preheat oven to Gas 3, 325°F, 160°C. Place the biscuits in a polythene bag and crush using a rolling pin. Finely chop the stem ginger. Melt the butter in a saucepan, then stir in crushed biscuits and ginger and mix together well. Place in the base of a loose-bottomed 8 in/20.5 cm cake tin and press down firmly with the back of a spoon. Leave the base to chill while preparing the filling.

Put the cream cheese in a large mixing bowl. Add the caster sugar and beat well, making sure that the mixture is smooth and free from lumps. Gradually add the beaten eggs, beating them in well. Add the vanilla essence. Pour mixture over the chilled biscuit base, smoothing the top. Bake on the centre shelf for 45-55 mins or until lightly set. Turn the oven off and leave in until the oven is cool. Remove, leave to cool for a further 30 mins then chill overnight in the fridge.

The next day, cut the apricots in half and remove the stones. Dissolve the sugar in ¼ pint/150 ml water then boil gently for 5 mins. Stir in the Grand Marnier then place the apricots in the syrup. Poach gently for 5-10 mins or until soft. Drain them thoroughly and remove the skins. Leave until completely cold.

Remove chilled cheesecake from the tin by placing the base on top of a clean large can, then carefully pull the tin down and gently slide it off the base and place on a serving plate. Arrange the cold, drained apricots on top of the cheesecake. Place some halved slices of kiwi fruit in the centre and top with an apricot half. Decorate edge with slices of kiwi fruit to add the finishing touch.

HANDY TIP

Arrange fruits on top and outside edge so that you can slice between them, to make it easier to serve the cheesecake.

1. Crush the biscuits finely, taking care not to split the polythene bag

2. Add crushed biscuits and ginger to melted butter, mixing well

3. Press biscuit mixture down firmly with back of spoon to flatten

4. Add the beaten eggs a little at a time, beating thoroughly

5. Place cheesecake on top of a large tin can before removing base

6. Arrange cooled apricots and kiwi fruit on cheesecake as shown

SHERRY TRIFLE

Light sponge cakes laced with sherry, covered with fruit and a creamy custard, topped with lashings of whipped cream. That's what makes this sherry trifle so delightful. Make two and freeze one for that special occasion.

Calories per portion: 555   **SERVES 6**

I pkt trifle sponge cakes
6 tbsp raspberry jam
6-8 tbsp medium dry sherry
14 oz/397g can fruit cocktail
I pint/600 ml milk
3 tbsp plain flour
2 eggs, size 3
I oz/25 g caster sugar
½ tsp vanilla essence
½ -I oz/15-25 g butter
½ pint/300 ml whipping cream
6 glacé cherries, halved
I oz/25 g flaked almonds

Cut the sponges evenly in half, spread with the raspberry jam and sandwich together. Place in the base of a glass serving dish, arranging the cakes so that the base of the dish is completely covered. If necessary, cut the sponge cakes in half so that there are no gaps.

Pour the sherry evenly over the sponge cakes. Drain the can of fruit, reserving 2-3 tbsp of the juice. Arrange the fruit over the cakes and pour the juice over. The sponge cakes should be well moistened but not swimming in excess liquid. If necessary, use less sherry or juice depending on how potent you want the trifle to be. Leave the soaked sponge cakes to one side while you are preparing the custard.

Heat the milk to blood heat (you can test this by dipping a clean finger into the milk – it should feel the same temperature as your finger).

Meanwhile, place the flour in a bowl, add the eggs and beat with a wooden spoon. Gradually stir in the warm milk and return the mixture to the pan. Heat gently until thickened.

At this stage it is very important to stir continuously to prevent the custard from becoming lumpy. If lumps do appear once the custard has thickened, strain it through a fine sieve. When the custard has thickened, cook for I min, remove from the heat then beat in the sugar, vanilla essence and butter. Beat until the butter has melted then pour over the sponge cakes and fruit. Leave until cooled. Place the trifle in the fridge or a cool place until the custard is completely cold.

Whip the cream until it is stiff and standing in soft peaks. Spoon into a piping bag fitted with a star nozzle and pipe a pattern across the top. Decorate the top with halved glacé cherries and flaked almonds.

1. Spread the halved sponge cakes with jam. Use to line the base of the dish

2. Moisten sponge cakes with sherry. Use extra sherry or fruit juice if liked

3. Spoon fruit over in an even layer. For a change, vary fruit and jam used

4. Beat eggs into flour. Heat milk to blood heat then stir into egg mixture

5. Remove thickened custard from heat. Beat in sugar, vanilla essence and butter

6. When custard is completely cold, whip cream until thick then pipe over top

TIRAMISU

When the occasion calls for an extra special treat, or even when you just want to spoil the family this stunning Italian dessert fits the menu perfectly. A combination of creamy cheese, sponge biscuits and a wicked hint of brandy, it's irresistible.

Calories per portion: 793

SERVES 4

2 egg yolks, size 3

2 tbsp caster sugar

2 tsp vanilla sugar, or ½ tsp
vanilla essence, plus 2 tsp
caster sugar

14 oz/400 g mascarpone cheese

2 tbsp brandy or coffee liqueur

4 tbsp strong black coffee

20 sponge finger biscuits

2 tsp cocoa powder, sieved

FOR THE MOCHA CREAM:

2 oz/50 g plain chocolate

1 tbsp coffee essence

¼ pint/150 ml double cream

1 tsp icing sugar, sieved

chocolate coffee beans
to decorate

Place the egg yolks, caster sugar and vanilla sugar – or vanilla essence and the 2 tsp caster sugar – in a mixing bowl. Whisk until the mixture is thick and creamy. Add 2 tbsp mascarpone cheese to the whisked mixture and fold in gently. Gradually add the remaining cheese, folding it in gently to form a smooth, thick cream.

Place the brandy, or the coffee liqueur, and coffee in a shallow dish. Dip the sponge finger biscuits into the coffee for a couple of seconds. The biscuits need to absorb the flavour of the coffee but still remain firm enough to prevent them disintegrating, so only dip a few biscuits in the coffee at a time as you begin to assemble the dessert.

In either four individual serving dishes or one large bowl, arrange alternate layers of biscuits and cheese mixture, finishing with a layer of the cheese mixture. Dust with the sieved cocoa powder, then chill in the fridge until set.

Meanwhile, make the mocha cream.

Break the chocolate into small pieces, then place chocolate and coffee essence in a heatproof bowl over a pan of gently simmering water. Ensure that the bottom of the bowl does not touch the water. Stir until the chocolate is smooth. Remove from the pan and leave to cool for 5 mins.

Whip the cream until just beginning to form soft peaks, then gradually fold it into the cooled melted chocolate. Cover and chill for 30 mins.

Just before serving, top the set Tiramisu with spoonfuls of the mocha cream and dust lightly with icing sugar. Decorate with chocolate coffee beans.·

H A N D Y   T I P

For a change, decorate with
brandy-flavoured whipped cream.

1. Place the egg yolks and sugars in a mixing bowl and whisk until creamy

2. Add 2 tbsp mascarpone cheese to the whisked mixture and fold in gently

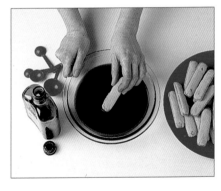

3. Place the brandy or coffee liqueur in a shallow dish and dip in the sponge fingers

4. Arrange alternate layers of biscuits and cheese mixture in serving dishes

5. Gradually fold the whipped cream into the cooled melted chocolate

6. Top set Tiramisu with spoonfuls of mocha cream, then dust with icing sugar

CHRISTMAS PUDDING

Make this deliciously light Christmas pudding, laden with dried fruit and flavoured with brandy a month in advance and give it time to mature. Using breadcrumbs instead of suet makes it healthier and also ideal for vegetarians.

Calories per portion: 698   SERVES 8

8 oz/225 g butter or margarine

8 oz/225 g muscovado sugar

3 eggs, size 3, beaten

4 tbsp golden syrup

grated rind and juice 1 lemon

8 oz/225 g fresh brown breadcrumbs

1 tsp ground cinnamon

1 tsp ground nutmeg

1 tsp ground ginger

8 oz/225 g sultanas

8 oz/225 g seedless raisins

8 oz/225 g currants

4 oz/100 g cut mixed peel

4 oz/100 g self-raising wholemeal flour

3 fl oz/85 ml brandy, sherry or fruit juice

Cream butter or margarine and sugar together until light and fluffy. Gradually beat in the eggs, syrup, grated rind and lemon juice. Stir in fruit, mixed peel, then flour and brandy, sherry or fruit juice. Stir in the breadcrumbs, then spices, ensuring that they are thoroughly mixed in. Cover the bowl and leave to stand overnight.

Next day cut out two small rounds of greaseproof paper to fit the base of two 2 pint/1.2 litre pudding basins. Grease basins lightly. Stir the mixture with a wooden spoon and make a wish! If you want to put in little Christmas novelties, now's the time, but make sure that they are suitable. DON'T use our present day coinage, they are not suitable – coins must be silver.

Divide the mixture between the two pudding basins to within 1½ in/4 cm of the top. Cover with either grease-proof paper and a pudding cloth or a double sheet of tin foil. Tie cloth securely or fold the tin foil firmly under rim. Place in top of a steamer and place over a pan of gently simmering water and steam for 6 hrs (top up with boiling water as necessary). Allow to cool, then recover and store in a cool dark place until required.

Before serving, steam for 2-3 hrs, then serve with brandy butter or cream and caster sugar. The earlier you make your pudding, the better, as this gives the pudding time to mature.

HANDY TIPS

Place a cut lemon in the base of the steamer – this will prevent the pan from turning black. For a delicious brandy butter, cream 3 oz/75 g unsalted butter with 5 oz/150 g caster sugar, then gradually beat in 3-4 tbsp of brandy. Cover and freeze if making in advance. This will keep in the fridge for up to one week.

1. Gradually add the beaten eggs to the creamed butter and sugar mixture a little at a time

2. Stir in the dried fruit and chopped mixed peel, ensuring they are thoroughly mixed in

3. Stir in the fresh brown breadcrumbs to create a much lighter pudding, ensuring they are well mixed in

4. Next day, divide the mixture between the prepared pudding basins to within 1½ in/4 cm of the rim, smoothing the top

5. Make a pleat in the tin foil to allow for expansion, use a long strip of foil for easy removal

6. Place the pudding in the top of the steamer, over a pan of gently simmering water and steam for 6 hrs

ICED ORANGE BOWL

This unusual, stunning dessert is a true masterpiece – an ice bowl, filled with juicy, tangy oranges, covered with smooth, golden caramel and decorated with fresh flowers.

Calories per portion: 208
SERVES 4

FOR THE ICE BOWL:
approx 36 ice cubes
fresh flowers and foliage
FOR THE CARAMELIZED
   ORANGES:
6 large oranges
4 tbsp Cointreau
4 oz/100 g caster sugar
mint sprigs, to decorate

Before you start, prepare a large enough space in your freezer for a 3 pint/1.7 litre glass bowl to stand upright, without tipping over. Adjust the freezer to rapid freeze.

Place a few ice cubes in the base of a 3 pint/1.7 litre glass bowl (one that's suitable for freezing – not a crystal glass bowl!). Next, place a 1½ pint./900 ml glass bowl on top of the ice cubes and decide where you'd like to position the flowers. Then break off the flower heads and small pieces of foliage and arrange in between the two bowls, wedging in position with ice cubes. Continue until you have filled the space between the bowls with flowers and ice cubes. Weigh down the smaller bowl by placing some heavy weights (about 1½ lb/675 g in total) inside it. Carefully pour sufficient cold water in between the two bowls to cover the flowers and ice cubes completely. Place the bowls in the freezer for at least 3 hrs, until frozen solid.

When completely frozen, remove the bowls from the freezer and return the freezer to its usual setting. Remove the weights from the smaller bowl, then

using a hot damp cloth, rub the inside of the smaller bowl until it loosens sufficiently for you to remove it.

Place the larger bowl in a sink or washing-up bowl, half-filled with hot water for 10 secs, taking care not to flood the centre. Slip out the ice bowl from the glass bowl. (You may need to repeat this process if it doesn't work the first time.) Place ice bowl on a freezer-proof plate. Return to the freezer until required.

To prepare caramelized oranges, carefully peel the oranges, using a small sharp knife, ensuring that none of the bitter white pith remains. Slice the oranges thinly, place in a bowl and pour the Cointreau over the fruit.

Place the caster sugar in a heavy-based saucepan with 8 tbsp water. Heat gently, stirring occasionally, until the sugar dissolves. Increase the heat, then boil the sugar syrup until it bubbles and turns golden brown.

Remove from the heat instantly and dip the base of the pan into cold water to stop the caramel cooking and to cool it quickly.

Remove the prepared ice bowl from the freezer and fill with the oranges, then drizzle the caramel over. Serve decorated with mint sprigs.

HANDY TIP

As an alternative, fill the ice bowl with scoops of ice cream.

1. Place a few ice cubes in a 3 pint/1.7 litre bowl. Place 1½ pint/900 ml bowl on top

2. Arrange flower heads and foliage in between bowls; wedge with ice cubes

3. Place weights inside smaller bowl, cover flowers with water, then freeze

4. Using a hot, damp cloth, rub the inside of the small bowl until it loosens

5. Carefully peel the oranges, ensuring none of the bitter white pith remains

6. Boil the sugar syrup in a pan until it bubbles and turns golden brown

CREPES SUZETTES

Wonderfully light pancakes, flavoured with lemon and orange butter, then flamed in brandy, make this classic dessert. Just follow this easy step-by-step recipe for perfect results – and serve up a delicious extra-special treat.

Calories per portion: 221   **SERVES 12**

4 oz/100 g plain flour
pinch of salt
3 eggs, size 3
8 fl oz/250 ml milk
1 oz/25 g butter, melted
4 oz/100 g butter, preferably
    unsalted, softened
3 oz/75 g icing sugar
grated rind of 1 lemon
grated rind and juice of 1 orange
2-3 tbsp Cointreau
1½ oz/40 g clarified butter or
    1-2 tbsp oil for frying
2-3 tbsp brandy
orange zest to decorate

Sieve the flour and salt into a mixing bowl, make a well in the centre, then break in the eggs. Using a balloon whisk, whisk flour into eggs, gradually drawing in flour from the sides of the bowl. Adding the milk, a little at a time, continue whisking until a smooth batter is formed. Then whisk in the melted butter. Leave for 30 mins (this will help the starch in the flour to soften and

expand in the liquid, resulting in a lighter crêpe).

Place softened butter in a bowl. Sieve icing sugar, add to butter. Beat until pale and creamy. Add lemon and orange rind, together with 2 tbsp orange juice. Beat well, then gradually beat in the remaining orange juice and the Cointreau. Cover and reserve.

When you are ready to cook the crêpes, heat a small knob of clarified butter or 1 tsp oil in a non-stick crêpe pan or small frying pan. When the pan is hot, swirl the melted butter or oil carefully around the pan, then pour off any excess. Pour 2 tbsp batter into the pan, again swirling the pan gently to allow the mixture to cover the base. Cook for 2-3 mins, or until the crêpe has set and is beginning to come away from the sides of the pan. Using a palette knife or spatula, turn the crêpe over and cook for a further 2 mins, or until the crêpe is cooked through and pale golden brown in colour.

Repeat until all the batter has been

used. Stack the crêpes on a plate with sheets of greaseproof or baking parchment between them. Keep the crêpes warm.

When ready to serve, fold four crêpes into quarters. Melt 2½ oz/65 g of the orange and lemon butter in a non-coated pan (it's inadvisable to flambé in a coated pan) and add crêpes. Heat through, spooning butter over. Pour in a little brandy, allow to heat through gently, then remove pan from heat and carefully ignite. Once the flames have subsided, decorate the crêpes with orange zest and serve. Repeat until all the crêpes have been used.

1. Sieve the flour and salt into a mixing bowl, break in the eggs, then whisk

2. Cream the butter and icing sugar together, beat in lemon and orange rind

3. After beating in the orange juice, add the Cointreau and beat until well mixed

4. Cook the crêpes until set, then, using a spatula, turn the pancake over

5. Melt the orange butter, fold the crêpes into quarters and add to the pan

6. After heating the crêpes through, add brandy, remove from heat and ignite

ICE CREAM BOMBE

Rich, luscious home-made strawberry, tutti frutti and chocolate ice cream, all frozen together to make a stunning dessert. It'll take a little longer to prepare than some puddings, but the taste is pure luxury, and it's worth every minute spent.

1. Lightly wash the strawberries and raspberries then blend to make a purée

2. For tutti frutti ice cream, chop glacé cherries, angelica, apricots and sultanas

3. Fold the strawberry and raspberry purée into the lightly whipped cream

**FOR THE STRAWBERRY
   ICE CREAM:**

12 oz/350 g strawberries

4 oz/100 g raspberries

juice of ½ lemon

10 oz/300 g icing sugar, sifted

½ pint/300 ml double cream

**FOR THE TUTTI FRUTTI
   ICE CREAM:**

4 oz/100 g sugar

9 fl oz/275 ml milk

1 vanilla pod

2 oz/50 g glacé cherries, washed

1 oz/25 g angelica, washed

2 oz/50 g no-need-to-soak
   apricots

2 oz/50 g sultanas

¼ pint/150 ml double cream

**FOR THE CHOCOLATE
   ICE CREAM:**

1 tbsp cornflour

¼ pint/150 ml milk

4 oz/100 g plain
   chocolate, melted

2 oz/50 g sugar

¼ pint/150 ml whipping cream

¼ pint/150 ml fromage frais

FOR THE STRAWBERRY SAUCE:

8 oz/225 g strawberries, washed

2 oz/50 g icing sugar

1 tbsp redcurrant jelly

2 tbsp whipped cream

Set freezer to rapid freeze. Have ready three clean, dry, freezable containers.

To make the strawberry ice cream, lightly wash the strawberries and raspberries, then pass through a food processor with the lemon juice to form a purée. Sieve to remove any pips. Stir icing sugar into purée. Whip cream until thick, fold in purée. Pour into container and freeze until just firm.

Dissolve the sugar for the tutti frutti ice cream in 3 tbsp water. Cool, then chill. Heat the milk with the vanilla pod to just below boiling point. Remove from heat, cover and leave to infuse for 15 mins. Discard the vanilla pod. Then chop the cherries, angelica, apricots and sultanas. Whip cream until thick, fold milk, sugar syrup and fruit into cream, pour into container and freeze until just firm.

To make the chocolate ice cream, blend the cornflour with a little of the milk. Heat remainder of the milk then pour on to the cornflour. Cook over a gentle heat, stirring until mixture thickens. Remove from heat, stir in the melted chocolate and sugar. Leave to cool. Lightly whip the cream and fromage frais together, then stir in chocolate mixture. Pour into container. Freeze until firm.

When the strawberry ice cream is lightly frozen, spoon into a 3 pint/ 1.7 litre pudding basin and with the back of a spoon, mould over the base and up the sides. Return to freezer until firm.

Using the tutti frutti ice cream, mould over the strawberry ice cream, leaving a hollow in the centre for the chocolate. Freeze until firm.

Fill centre with the chocolate ice cream and smooth over to give a flat base. Return to freezer until solid.

To unmould the bombe, carefully run a knife round the inner edge of basin, invert on to serving plate and wrap a hot towel round. Leave a couple of mins, then remove towel and basin. Decorate the bombe with rosettes of cream and a few extra strawberries.

To make the strawberry sauce, place the strawberries, icing sugar and redcurrant jelly in a food processor, purée until smooth and then sieve to remove any pips.

HANDY TIP

Leave bombe in the fridge for 20 mins before serving. Return freezer to normal setting.

4. Smooth the strawberry ice cream up sides of basin using the back of a spoon

5. When the strawberry ice cream has frozen, spoon in the tutti frutti ice cream

6. Fill the remainder of the basin with the chocolate ice cream. Smooth top

FLOATING ISLANDS

When you want to serve something a little different, try this classic dessert. A smooth creamy custard with the subtle tang of cinnamon, topped with lightly poached meringues then drizzled with caramel syrup.

Calories per portion: 246

SERVES 4

¾ pint/450 ml semi-skimmed
milk
2 cinnamon sticks
4 egg yolks, size 3
1 egg, size 3
4 oz/100 g caster sugar

Place the milk in a pan. Tap the cinnamon sticks lightly with a rolling pin to bruise them slightly without breaking them completely, add to milk and bring to just below boiling point. Remove from the heat and leave to infuse for at least 30 mins then strain and discard the cinnamon sticks. Place the egg yolks into a bowl. Separate the whole egg and place the yolk with the other egg yolks. Place the white in a clean bowl (reserve for later). Whisk 1 oz/25 g of the sugar into the egg yolks then the strained milk. Pour into a heavy-based saucepan or into a double boiler, cook over a gentle heat, stirring throughout until the custard thickens and coats the back of a spoon. Pour into a serving bowl then chill in the fridge for at least 1 hr.

Whisk the egg white until stiff and standing in peaks, then gradually whisk in 1½ oz/40 g of the remaining sugar. Continue to whisk until the mixture is stiff and glossy and small peaks are made when the whisk is pulled away from the meringue.

Half fill a frying pan with cold water and bring to a gentle boil. Reduce heat so that the surface of the water is just moving. Using two spoons, shape the mixture into ovals then carefully place in the water. Poach for at least 5 mins or until meringues are set. Remove from the pan and drain on absorbent paper before arranging on top of the chilled custard.

Place the remaining 1½ oz/40 g of caster sugar in a heavy-based saucepan with 2 tsp of cold water. Place over a gentle heat and stir until dissolved. Increase the heat and boil steadily until a golden caramel coloured syrup is formed. Carefully drizzle a little caramel syrup over the top of each meringue then serve.

HANDY TIPS

You can vary the flavour of the custard by replacing the cinnamon sticks with a vanilla pod, or use ½ tsp vanilla essence. Try infusing the milk with the finely pared rind of an orange or lemon.

1. Place pan over a very gentle heat and cook, stirring throughout until the custard thickens and coats the back of a spoon

2. Whisk the egg white until stiff and standing in peaks, gradually whisk in the sugar, whisk until stiff

3. Half fill a frying pan with cold water, bring to a gentle boil then spoon in the shaped meringues

4. Remove the meringues from the pan and allow to drain thoroughly on absorbent paper

5. Dissolve remaining sugar in a heavy-based pan, bring to the boil, boil until a golden syrup is formed

6. Arrange drained meringues on top of the custard. Carefully drizzle a little of the syrup over the meringues, then serve

CHARLOTTE RUSSE

Sugary biscuits, surrounding a delicious home-made custard filling, flavoured with pineapple, create this mouthwatering dessert which looks as good as it tastes. A superb ending to any meal.

½ pint/300 ml fresh apple juice

2 x ½ oz/15 g sachets gelatine

1 small star fruit

2-3 fresh strawberries

20 sponge finger biscuits

3 eggs, size 3, separated

3 oz/75 g caster sugar

7 fl oz/200 ml milk

7 oz/197g can pineapple chunks
   in natural juice

½ pint/300 ml whipping cream

frosted grapes to decorate (see
   handy tips)

Pour the apple juice into a clean pan and bring to boil. Switch off heat and sprinkle in one sachet gelatine. Whisk until completely dissolved. Allow to cool, then pour a thin layer into a 7 in/18 cm round cake tin and leave until the jelly is completely set.

Meanwhile, wash, then slice the star fruit thinly. Wash, dry and halve the strawberries. Dip fruit slices into remaining liquid jelly (if it has started to set, gently warm it through to melt it again). Using a skewer, arrange fruit in a decorative pattern over the set apple jelly. Allow the fruit to set, then pour in another ½ in/1.25 cm layer of liquid jelly on top.

Dip both sides of the sponge finger biscuits into the liquid jelly. Arrange biscuits, sugar-side out, around the edge of the tin. Leave until set.

Place the egg yolks and sugar in a bowl over a pan of gently simmering water. Whisk until pale and creamy. Remove from the heat. Warm the milk to blood heat, then beat into egg mixture. Strain into a clean pan and cook over a gentle heat, stirring throughout, until the mixture thickens and coats the back of a spoon. Strain into a clean bowl and leave to cool, stirring occasionally.

Dissolve the remaining packet of gelatine in 3 tbsp hot water and stir into cooled custard. Drain the pineapple and chop. Whip the cream until thick. Whisk the egg whites until stiff and in peaks. Gently fold the cream, pineapple and egg whites into custard mixture, then spoon over the set apple jelly, ensuring there are no air pockets.

Smooth the top and chill until set. When ready to serve, trim biscuits, if necessary, to the level of the filling. Dip base of tin quickly into hot water. Invert on a serving plate. Decorate with frosted grapes.

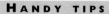

HANDY TIPS

To frost grapes, whisk one egg white until frothy. Wash and dry small bunches of grapes, dip them in egg white or water, then roll in caster sugar. Leave to dry. Other fruits, such as satsuma segments, strawberries and currants can also be frosted in this way. Use within two days. You can also frost edible flowers such as primroses and violets in this way.

1. Add the gelatine to the apple juice and whisk until completely dissolved

2. Using a skewer, arrange the dipped fruit on top of jelly in a decorative pattern

3. Dip the sponge biscuits in the liquid apple jelly and place around tin

4. Stir custard over a gentle heat until it coats the back of a spoon

5. Gently fold cream, pineapple and egg whites into the custard

6. Spoon custard and cream mixture over the set jelly. Smooth the top

CROQUEMBOUCHE

Choux buns, filled with
tasty crème pâtissière,
sitting on a shortcake base,
decorated with a delicate
web of fine sugar.

Calories per portion: 611

SERVES 8

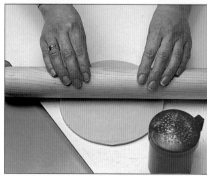

*1. On a lightly floured surface, roll out
shortcake dough to an 8 in/20.5 cm circle*

*2. Add flour to choux mixture, beat to
form a ball. Add beaten eggs, beat again*

*3. Place choux paste in a piping bag. Pipe
small rounds on a damp baking sheet*

FOR THE SHORTCAKE BASE:
6 oz/175 g plain flour
1½ oz/40 g caster sugar
3 oz/75 g butter or
  margarine, softened
1 egg, size 3
FOR THE CHOUX BUNS:
4 oz/100 g plain flour
3 oz/75 g butter
3 eggs, size 3, beaten
FOR THE CREME PATISSIERE:
3 eggs, size 3
2 oz/50 g caster sugar
3 tbsp plain flour
3 tbsp cornflour
¾ pint/450 ml milk, warmed
1 teaspoon vanilla essence
1 oz/25 g butter
FOR THE CARAMEL:
8 oz/225 g caster sugar

Preheat the oven to Gas 4, 350°F, 180°C. To make the base, sieve the flour into a bowl, then add the caster sugar. Cut the fat into small pieces and rub into the flour and sugar until the mixture resembles breadcrumbs. Bind together with the egg. Knead dough lightly, then roll out on a lightly floured surface to an 8 in/20.5 cm circle. Place on a baking sheet, prick lightly, then bake for 20-25 mins, or until pale golden. Remove from oven, cool slightly, then transfer to a wire cooling rack.

To make the choux buns, increase the oven temperature to Gas 6, 400°F, 200°C. Sieve the flour. Place the butter in a pan with 7 fl oz/200 ml water and bring to the boil, stirring occasionally. Remove from the heat, then add the flour. Beat vigorously until the mixture forms a ball. Add the beaten eggs, a little at a time, beating well after each addition. Place mixture in a piping bag with a ½ in/1.25 cm plain nozzle, then pipe small rounds on to a damp baking sheet. Bake for 15-20 mins, or until golden. Remove buns from the oven, make a small slit in each one, then return to the oven for 5 mins. Cool and reserve.

To make crème pâtissière, beat eggs and caster sugar together and sieve flours. Beat the flours into the egg

mixture until smooth, then gradually beat in the milk. Strain, then place in a pan over a gentle heat and cook, stirring continuously, until thickened and smooth. Remove from the heat and beat in the vanilla essence and butter. Leave covered until cold.

To make caramel, dissolve the caster sugar in ½ pint/300 ml water in a heavy-based saucepan. Bring to boil and boil until a light caramel forms. Place base of pan in cold water.

To assemble, fill buns with crème pâtissière. Dip base and outer side of each bun into the caramel, place around edge of shortcake base, then on top of each other, building up to form a pyramid.

Reheat the caramel slightly, then spin strands by dipping a spoon in the caramel, placing a fork on top, then pulling the two apart. As the caramel cools, strands will form between the spoon and fork. Use to decorate the Croquembouche. Serve with a selection of fresh fruit.

HANDY TIP

Make the base and choux buns earlier, freeze until required. When ready to use, thaw then crisp the choux buns in oven for 5 mins, fill and proceed as above.

4. Dip the filled choux buns into caramel, then arrange on the shortcake base

5. Continue dipping buns into caramel and building them up to form a pyramid

6. Dip a spoon in the caramel, place a fork on top, pull apart to spin strands

CHRISTMAS BOMBE

For something a little lighter than the traditional puddings this Christmas or at any time, try this sensational dessert. Tutti frutti ice cream and Raspberry Crush encased in plain chocolate, served with a creamy white chocolate sauce.

Calories per portion: 576 **SERVES 8**

1¾ pint/1 litre tub tutti frutti ice cream
FOR THE RASPBERRY CRUSH:
8 oz/225 g frozen raspberries (do not thaw)
8 fl oz/250 ml buttermilk
2-3 tbsp icing sugar
8 oz/225 g plain chocolate
FOR THE SAUCE:
4 oz/100 g white chocolate
½ oz/15 g butter
¼ pint/150 ml double cream
1-2 tbsp brandy
mint leaves to decorate

Set freezer to rapid freeze. Using a metal spoon, press the ice cream into a 2½ pint/1.5 litre bombe mould or pudding basin, forming a well in the centre. Cover and freeze for 30 mins.

Meanwhile, prepare the Raspberry Crush. Reserving 2 oz/50 g of the frozen raspberries for decoration, place remainder in a food processor or blender. Whilst crushing the raspberries pour in the buttermilk and enough icing sugar to taste, until a soft, icy mixture is formed. Pile this mixture into the centre of the ice cream lined mould. Cover and freeze for 15 mins.

Place bombe in a bowl of hot water for 10 secs and invert on to a greaseproof paper lined plate to remove from mould. Re-freeze for 15 mins whilst preparing the plain chocolate casing.

Break the plain chocolate into pieces and place in a heatproof bowl over a pan of simmering water until melted. Beat until glossy and smooth.

Remove bombe from freezer and spoon over the chocolate, ensuring all the ice cream is covered – work quickly to prevent ice cream melting too much. Refreeze for 30 mins whilst making the sauce.

Break white chocolate into pieces and place in a heatproof bowl over a pan of simmering water until melted. Remove from heat and beat in the butter, and gradually beat in the cream. Stir in brandy to taste.

Remove bombe from freezer, allow to thaw slowly in the fridge for 20 mins before serving.

Decorate the bombe with the reserved raspberries and mint leaves. Run the blade of a sharp knife under hot water and slice the bombe to serve, accompanied by the white chocolate sauce.

1. Using a metal spoon, press the ice cream into a 2½ pint/1.5 litre bombe mould or pudding basin

2. Blend raspberries. While blending, pour in buttermilk and icing sugar until a soft icy mixture is formed

3. Pile Raspberry Crush into the centre of the ice cream mould. Cover and freeze for 15 mins

4. Place mould in hot water for 10 secs and invert on to a greaseproof paper-lined plate

5. Working quickly spoon melted plain chocolate over the bombe ensuring all the ice cream is covered

6. Melt white chocolate, beat in the fat, then gradually beat in the cream. Stir in the brandy to taste

ACKNOWLEDGEMENTS

All photography by John Elliot.
Except for: Sultana Cheesecake, Marbled Pudding, Tarte Tatin, Orange Soufflé,
Lemon Tart, Pears in Red Wine by Karl Adamson
Crème Caramel and Mount Vesuvius by David Armstrong
Iced Orange Bowl and Pear and Almond Tart by Ian 'O' Leary
Blackberry Charlotte and Christmas Bombe by Ken Field
Tiramisu by Ferguson Hill

Gina Steer would like to thank Kathryn Hawkins and Jenny Brightman for their help in
assisting in some of the photography, styling and recipe testing.